studysync®

Reading & Writing Companion

A Moral Compass

studysync

studysync.com

STUDENT GUIDE

GETTING STARTED

Welcome to the StudySync Reading and Writing Companion! In this booklet, you will find a collection of readings based on the theme of the unit you are studying. As you work through the readings, you will be asked to answer questions and perform a variety of tasks designed to help you closely analyze and understand each text selection. Read on for an explanation of each section of this booklet.

CORE ELA TEXTS

In each Core ELA Unit you will read texts and text excerpts that share a common theme, despite their different genres, time periods, and authors. Each reading encourages a closer look with questions and a short writing assignment.

1 INTRODUCTION

An Introduction to each text provides historical context for your reading as well as information about the author. You will also learn about the genre of the excerpt and the year in which it was written.

2 FIRST READ

During your first reading of each excerpt, you should just try to get a general idea of the content and message of the reading. Don't worry if there are parts you don't understand or words that are unfamiliar to you. You'll have an opportunity later to dive deeper into the text.

3 NOTES

Many times, while working through the activities after each text, you will be asked to **annotate** or **make annotations** about what you are reading. This means that you should highlight or underline words in the text and use the "Notes" column to make comments or jot down any questions you may have. You may also want to note any unfamiliar vocabulary words here.

4 THINK QUESTIONS

These questions will ask you to start thinking critically about the text, asking specific questions about its purpose, and making connections to your prior knowledge and reading experiences. To answer these questions, you should go back to the text and draw upon specific evidence that you find there to support your responses. You will also begin to explore some of the more challenging vocabulary words used in the excerpt.

5 CLOSE READ & FOCUS QUESTIONS

After you have completed the First Read, you will then be asked to go back and read the excerpt more closely and critically. Before you begin your Close Read, you should read through the Focus Questions to get an idea of the concepts you will want to focus on during your second reading. You should work through the Focus Questions by making annotations, highlighting important concepts, and writing notes or questions in the "Notes" column. Depending on instructions from your teacher, you may need to respond online or use a separate piece of paper to start expanding on your thoughts and ideas.

6 WRITING PROMPT

Your study of each excerpt or selection will end with a writing assignment. To complete this assignment, you should use your notes, annotations, and answers to both the Think and Focus Questions. Be sure to read the prompt carefully and address each part of it in your writing assignment.

ENGLISH LANGUAGE DEVELOPMENT TEXTS

The English Language Development texts and activities take a closer look at the language choices that authors make to communicate their ideas. Individual and group activities will help develop your understanding of each text.

1 REREAD

After you have completed the First Read, you will have two additional opportunities to revisit portions of the excerpt more closely. The directions for each reread will specify which paragraphs or sections you should focus on.

2 USING LANGUAGE

These questions will ask you to analyze the author's use of language and conventions in the text. You may be asked to write in sentence frames, fill in a chart, or you may simply choose between multiple-choice options. To answer these questions, you should read the exercise carefully and go back in the text as necessary to accurately complete the activity.

3 MEANINGFUL INTERACTIONS & SELF-ASSESSMENT RUBRIC

After each reading, you will participate in a group activity or discussion with your peers. You may be provided speaking frames to guide your discussions or writing frames to support your group work. To complete these activities, you should revisit the excerpt for textual evidence and support. When you finish, use the Self-Assessment Rubric to evaluate how well you participated and collaborated.

EXTENDED WRITING PROJECT

The Extended Writing Project is your opportunity to explore the theme of each unit in a longer written work. You will draw information from your readings, research, and own life experiences to complete the assignment.

1 WRITING PROJECT

After you have read all of the unit text selections, you will move on to a writing project. Each project will guide you through the process of writing an argumentative, narrative, informative, or literary analysis essay. Student models and graphic organizers will provide guidance and help you organize your thoughts as you plan and write your essay. Throughout the project, you will also study and work on specific writing skills to help you develop different portions of your writing.

2 WRITING PROCESS STEPS

There are five steps in the writing process: **Prewrite**, **Plan**, **Draft**, **Revise**, and **Edit**, **Proofread**, **and Publish**. During each step, you will form and shape your writing project so that you can effectively express your ideas. Lessons focus on one step at a time, and you will have the chance to receive feedback from your peers and teacher.

3 WRITING SKILLS

Each Writing Skill lesson focuses on a specific strategy or technique that you will use during your writing project. The lessons begin by analyzing a student model or mentor text, and give you a chance to learn and practice the skill on its own. Then, you will have the opportunity to apply each new skill to improve the writing in your own project.

A Moral Compass

TEXTS

4   **Abuela Invents the Zero**
     FICTION *Judith Ortiz Cofer*

10   **Home**
     FICTION *Anton Chekhov*

21   **A Celebration of Grandfathers**
     NON-FICTION *Rudolfo Anaya*

29   **Mother to Son**
     POETRY *Langston Hughes*

33   **Little Women**
     FICTION *Louisa May Alcott*

40   **The Adventures of Tom Sawyer (Chapter 2)**
     FICTION *Mark Twain*

46   **Born Worker**
     FICTION *Gary Soto*

58   **Ode to Thanks**
     POETRY *Pablo Neruda*

63 The Little Boy Lost/The Little Boy Found
POETRY *William Blake*

67 A Poison Tree
POETRY *William Blake*

71 Mandatory Volunteer Work for Teenagers
NON-FICTION *Point/Counterpoint*

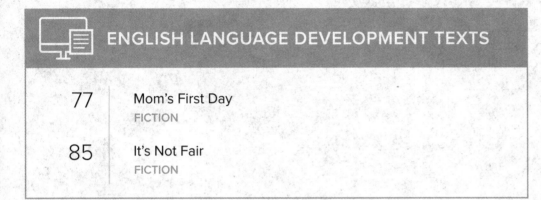

ENGLISH LANGUAGE DEVELOPMENT TEXTS

77 Mom's First Day
FICTION

85 It's Not Fair
FICTION

EXTENDED WRITING PROJECT

94 Extended Writing Project: Literary Analysis

99 Extended Writing Project: Prewrite

101 SKILL: Thesis Statement

103 SKILL: Organize Argumentative Writing

107 SKILL: Supporting Details

110 Extended Writing Project: Plan

113 SKILL: Introductions

116 SKILL: Conclusions

119 Extended Writing Project: Draft

121 Extended Writing Project: Style

125 Extended Writing Project: Revise

127 SKILL: Sources and Citations

131 Extended Writing Project: Edit, Proofread, and Publish

135

Text Fulfillment
through
StudySync

Copyright © BookheadEd Learning, LLC

ABUELA INVENTS THE ZERO

FICTION
Judith Ortiz Cofer
1996

INTRODUCTION

Judith Ortiz Cofer's writing reflects the differences between her two childhood homes; one on the island of Puerto Rico and one in a *barrio* (neighborhood) on the mainland. In this short story, Constancia is a teenager whose *abuela* (grandmother) comes to visit her in New Jersey. Caught between her American and Puerto Rican identities, Constancia feels embarrassed by the "bizarre" behavior of her *abuela* at church, and hides her face in shame. Later, she is left to contemplate the meaning of "zero."

"I realize to my horror that my grandmother is lost."

FIRST READ

1   "You made me feel like a zero, like a nothing," she says in Spanish, *un cero, nada*. She is trembling, an angry little old woman lost in a heavy winter coat that belongs to my mother. And I end up being sent to my room, like I was a child, to think about my grandmother's idea of math.

2   It all began with Abuela coming up from the Island for a visit—her first time in the United States. My mother and father paid her way here so that she wouldn't die without seeing snow, though if you asked me, and nobody has, the dirty slush in this city is not worth the price of a ticket. But I guess she deserves some kind of award for having had ten kids and survived to tell about it. My mother is the youngest of the bunch. Right up to the time when we're supposed to pick up the old lady at the airport, my mother is telling me stories about how hard times were for *la familia* on *la isla*, and how *la abuela* worked night and day to support them after their father died of a heart attack. I'd die of a heart attack too if I had a troop like that to support. Anyway, I had seen her only three or four times in my entire life, whenever we would go for somebody's funeral. I was born here and I have lived in this building all my life. But when Mami says, "Connie, please be nice to Abuela. She doesn't have too many years left. Do you promise me, Constancia?"—when she uses my full name, I know she means business. So I say, "Sure." Why wouldn't I be nice? I'm not a monster, after all.

3   So we go to Kennedy to get *la abuela*, and she is the last to come out of the airplane, on the arm of the cabin attendant, all wrapped up in a black shawl. He hands her over to my parents like she was a package sent airmail. It is January, two feet of snow on the ground, and she's wearing a shawl over a thick black dress. That's just the start.

4   Once home, she refuses to let my mother buy her a coat because it's a waste of money for the two weeks she'll be in *el Polo Norte,* as she calls New

Please note that excerpts and passages in the StudySync® library and this workbook are intended as touchstones to generate interest in an author's work. The excerpts and passages do not substitute for the reading of entire texts, and StudySync® strongly recommends that students seek out and purchase the whole literary or informational work in order to experience it as the author intended. Links to online resellers are available in our digital library. In addition, complete works may be ordered through an authorized reseller by filling out and returning to StudySync® the order form enclosed in this workbook.

Reading & Writing Companion   **5**

Jersey, the North Pole. So since she's only four feet eleven inches tall, she walks around in my mother's big black coat looking ridiculous. I try to walk far behind them in public so that no one will think we're together. I plan to stay very busy the whole time she's with us so that I won't be asked to take her anywhere, but my plan is ruined when my mother comes down with the flu and Abuela absolutely *has* to attend Sunday mass or her soul will be eternally damned. She's more Catholic than the Pope. My father decides that he should stay home with my mother and that I should escort *la abuela* to church. He tells me this on Saturday night as I'm getting ready to go out to the mall with my friends.

5   "No way," I say.

6   I go for the car keys on the kitchen table: he usually leaves them there for me
7   on Friday and Saturday nights. He beats me to them. "No way," he says, pocketing them and grinning at me.

8   Needless to say, we come to a **compromise** very quickly. I do have a responsibility to Sandra and Anita, who don't drive yet. There is a Harley-Davidson fashion show at Brookline Square that we *cannot* miss.

9   "The mass in Spanish is at ten sharp tomorrow morning, entiendes?" My father is dangling the car keys in front of my nose and pulling them back when I try to reach for them. He's really enjoying himself.

10   "I understand. Ten o'clock. I'm out of here." I pry his fingers off the key ring. He knows that I'm late, so he makes it just a little difficult. Then he laughs. I run out of our apartment before he changes his mind. I have no idea what I'm getting myself into.

11   Sunday morning I have to walk two blocks on dirty snow to retrieve the car. I warm it up for Abuela as instructed by my parents, and drive it to the front of our building. My father walks her by the hand in baby steps on the slippery snow. The sight of her little head with a bun on top of it sticking out of that huge coat makes me want to run back into my room and get under the covers. I just hope that nobody I know sees us together. I'm dreaming, of course. The mass is packed with people from our block. It's a holy day of **obligation** and everyone I ever met is there.

12   I have to help her climb the steps, and she stops to take a deep breath after each one, then I lead her down the aisle so that everybody can see me with my bizarre grandmother. If I were a good Catholic, I'm sure I'd get some **purgatory** time taken off for my sacrifice. She is walking as slow as Captain Cousteau exploring the bottom of the sea, looking around, taking her sweet time. Finally she chooses a pew, but she wants to sit in the other end. It's like she had a spot picked out for some unknown reason, and although it's the

NOTES

most inconvenient seat in the house, that's where she has to sit. So we squeeze by all the people already sitting there, saying, "Excuse me, please, *con permiso,* pardon me," getting annoyed looks the whole way. By the time we settle in, I'm drenched in sweat. I keep my head down like I'm praying so as not to see or be seen. She is praying loud, in Spanish, and singing hymns at the top of her creaky voice.

13   I ignore her when she gets up with a hundred other people to go take communion. I'm actually praying hard now—that this will all be over soon. But the next time I look up, I see a black coat dragging around and around the church, stopping here and there so a little gray head can peek out like a **periscope** on a submarine. There are giggles in the church, and even the priest has frozen in the middle of a blessing, his hands above his head like he is about to lead the congregation in a set of jumping jacks.

14   I realize to my horror that my grandmother is lost. She can't find her way back to the pew. I am so embarrassed that even though the woman next to me is shooting daggers at me with her eyes, I just can't move to go get her. I put my hands over my face like I'm praying, but it's really to hide my burning cheeks. I would like for her to disappear. I just know that on Monday my friends, and my enemies, in the barrio will have a lot of **senile**-grandmother jokes to tell in front of me. I am frozen to my seat. So the same woman who wants me dead on the spot does it for me. She makes a big deal out of getting up and hurrying to get Abuela.

15   The rest of the mass is a blur. All I know is that my grandmother kneels the whole time with her hands over *her* face. She doesn't speak to me on the way home, and she doesn't let me help her walk, even though she almost falls a couple of times.

16   When we get to the apartment, my parents are at the kitchen table, where my mother is trying to eat some soup. They can see right away that something is wrong. Then Abuela points her finger at me like a judge passing a sentence on a criminal. She says in Spanish, "You made me feel like a zero, like a nothing." Then she goes to her room.

17   I try to explain what happened. "I don't understand why she's so upset. She just got lost and wandered around for a while," I tell them. But it sounds lame, even to my own ears. My mother gives me a look that makes me cringe and goes in to Abuela's room to get her version of the story. She comes out with tears in her eyes.

18   "Your grandmother says to tell you that of all the hurtful things you can do to a person, the worst is to make them feel as if they are worth nothing."

Please note that excerpts and passages in the StudySync® library and this workbook are intended as touchstones to generate interest in an author's work. The excerpts and passages do not substitute for the reading of entire texts, and StudySync® strongly recommends that students seek out and purchase the whole literary or informational work in order to experience it as the author intended. Links to online resellers are available in our digital library. In addition, complete works may be ordered through an authorized reseller by filling out and returning to StudySync® the order form enclosed in this workbook.

Reading & Writing Companion   **7**

NOTES

19 I can feel myself shrinking right there in front of her. But I can't bring myself to tell my mother that I think I understand how I made Abuela feel. I might be sent into the old lady's room to apologize, and it's not easy to admit you've been a jerk—at least, not right away with everybody watching. So I just sit there not saying anything.

20 My mother looks at me for a long time, like she feels sorry for me. Then she says, "You should know, Constancia, that if it wasn't for the old woman whose existence you don't seem to value, you and I would not be here."

21 That's when *I'm* sent to *my* room to consider a number I hadn't thought much about—until today.

"Abuela Invents the Zero" from *An Island Like You: Stories of the Barrio* by Judith Ortiz Cofer and published by Scholastic, Inc. Copyright (c) 1995 by Judith Ortiz Cofer. Reprinted with permission. All rights reserved.

THINK QUESTIONS CA-CCSS: CA.RL.8.1, CA.L.8.4a, CA.L.8.4b

1. Describe Constancia's relationship with Abuela prior to her grandmother's visit to New Jersey. Cite details from the text to support your response.

2. Refer to details from the text to explain why Constancia considers her grandmother to be, in her eyes, "ridiculous" and "bizarre."

3. How does Constancia respond when Abuela becomes lost in the church? Describe her reaction, and support your answer with textual evidence.

4. Use context to determine the meaning of the word **obligation** as it is used in paragraph 11 of "Abuela Invents the Zero." Write your definition of "obligation" and explain how you found it.

5. Remembering that the Greek prefix peri- means "around," use your understanding of the Greek prefix as well as context clues in "Abuela Invents the Zero" to determine the meaning of **periscope** in paragraph 13. Write your definition of "periscope."

CLOSE READ
CA-CCSS: CA.RL.8.1, CA.RL.8.2, CA.RL.8.3, CA.W.8.4, CA.W.8.5, CA.W.8.6, CA.W.8.10

Reread the short story "Abuela Invents the Zero." As you reread, complete the Focus Questions below. Then use your answers and annotations from the questions to help you complete the Writing Prompt.

FOCUS QUESTIONS

1. Before Abuela's arrival, which lines of dialogue in the story reveal that Constancia is unaware of the consequences her actions can have, and that Constancia's mother knows her daughter well and is trying to prevent any tension from occurring? Highlight evidence in the text and make annotations to support your answer.

2. Analyzing particular incidents in a story or drama can provide readers with details that point to the theme. Reread paragraphs 14 and 15 and highlight specific evidence that suggests how the incident at the church is a turning point in the relationship between Constancia and Abuela, and what it reveals about the theme.

3. Reread the last five paragraphs of the story. What information does the author include that suggests Constancia still doesn't fully realize how much her behavior has hurt her grandmother? Highlight evidence in the text that supports your answer.

4. Throughout the story, how does the author reveal the importance Constancia places on clothes and appearance, and how does this character trait serve to create a distance between grandmother and granddaughter? Highlight evidence in the text that supports your answer.

5. Compare and contrast Abuela with her granddaughter. What values do each of them have at the beginning of the story? How have their life experiences helped to shape their values? Highlight evidence in the text that supports your answer.

WRITING PROMPT

How does the theme of "Abuela Invents the Zero" help you understand a larger lesson about how life experiences can shape our values? Use the details you have compiled from examining the conflict between the characters, as well as the characters' thoughts, dialogue, feelings, and actions, to:

- identify the theme of the story
- analyze how it is developed over the course of the text

Remember to support your writing with evidence and inferences from the text.

Please note that excerpts and passages in the StudySync® library and this workbook are intended as touchstones to generate interest in an author's work. The excerpts and passages do not substitute for the reading of entire texts, and StudySync® strongly recommends that students seek out and purchase the whole literary or informational work in order to experience it as the author intended. Links to online resellers are available in our digital library. In addition, complete works may be ordered through an authorized reseller by filling out and returning to StudySync® the order form enclosed in this workbook.

Reading & Writing Companion

9

HOME

FICTION

Anton Chekhov
1887

INTRODUCTION

Anton Chekhov is one of Russia's most prized short story writers. He is known for his authentic and objective depictions of characters and situations and his humorous style. In this excerpt from Anton Chekhov's short story *Home*, a prosecutor discovers that his young son has been smoking, and uses the occasion to both teach the boy a lesson and muse on the nature of morality.

"I tell you, my boy, I don't love you, and you are no son of mine..."

 FIRST READ

1 "SOMEONE came from the Grigoryevs' to fetch a book, but I said you were not at home. The postman brought the newspaper and two letters. By the way, Yevgeny Petrovitch, I should like to ask you to speak to Seryozha. To-day, and the day before yesterday, I have noticed that he is smoking. When I began to expostulate with him, he put his fingers in his ears as usual, and sang loudly to drown my voice."

2 Yevgeny Petrovitch Bykovsky, the prosecutor of the circuit court, who had just come back from a session and was taking off his gloves in his study, looked at the governess as she made her report, and laughed.

3 "Seryozha smoking . . ." he said, shrugging his shoulders. "I can picture the little cherub with a cigarette in his mouth! Why, how old is he?"

4 "Seven. You think it is not important, but at his age smoking is a bad and pernicious habit, and bad habits ought to be eradicated in the beginning."

5 "Perfectly true. And where does he get the tobacco?"

6 "He takes it from the drawer in your table."

7 "Yes? In that case, send him to me."

8 When the governess had gone out, Bykovsky sat down in an arm-chair before his writing-table, shut his eyes, and fell to thinking. He pictured his Seryozha with a huge cigar, a yard long, in the midst of clouds of tobacco smoke, and this caricature made him smile; at the same time, the grave, troubled face of the governess called up memories of the long past, half-forgotten time when smoking aroused in his teachers and parents a strange, not quite intelligible horror. It really was horror. Children were mercilessly flogged and expelled

from school, and their lives were made a misery on account of smoking, though not a single teacher or father knew exactly what was the harm or sinfulness of smoking. Even very intelligent people did not **scruple** to wage war on a vice which they did not understand. Yevgeny Petrovitch remembered the head-master of the high school, a very cultured and good-natured old man, who was so appalled when he found a high-school boy with a cigarette in his mouth that he turned pale, immediately summoned an emergency committee of the teachers, and sentenced the sinner to expulsion. This was probably a law of social life: the less an evil was understood, the more fiercely and coarsely it was attacked.

9   "The prosecutor remembered two or three boys who had been expelled and their subsequent life, and could not help thinking that very often the punishment did a great deal more harm than the crime itself. The living organism has the power of rapidly adapting itself, growing accustomed and **inured** to any atmosphere whatever, otherwise man would be bound to feel at every moment what an irrational basis there often is underlying his rational activity, and how little of established truth and certainty there is even in work so responsible and so terrible in its effects as that of the teacher, of the lawyer, of the writer. . . .

10 And such light and **discursive** thoughts as visit the brain only when it is weary and resting began straying through Yevgeny Petrovitch's head; there is no telling whence and why they come, they do not remain long in the mind, but seem to glide over its surface without sinking deeply into it. For people who are forced for whole hours, and even days, to think by routine in one direction, such free private thinking affords a kind of comfort, an agreeable solace.

11 It was between eight and nine o'clock in the evening. Overhead, on the second storey, someone was walking up and down, and on the floor above that four hands were playing scales. The pacing of the man overhead who, to judge from his nervous step, was thinking of something harassing, or was suffering from toothache, and the monotonous scales gave the stillness of the evening a drowsiness that disposed to lazy reveries. In the nursery, two rooms away, the governess and Seryozha were talking.

12 "Pa-pa has come!" carolled the child. "Papa has co-ome. Pa! Pa! Pa!"

13 *"Votre père vous appelle, allez vite!"* cried the governess, shrill as a frightened bird. "I am speaking to you!"

14 "What am I to say to him, though?" Yevgeny Petrovitch wondered.

15 But before he had time to think of anything whatever his son Seryozha, a boy of seven, walked into the study.

16   He was a child whose sex could only have been guessed from his dress: weakly, white-faced, and fragile. He was limp like a hot-house plant, and everything about him seemed extraordinarily soft and tender: his movements, his curly hair, the look in his eyes, his velvet jacket.

17   "Good evening, papa!" he said, in a soft voice, clambering on to his father's knee and giving him a rapid kiss on his neck. "Did you send for me?"

18   "Excuse me, Sergey Yevgenitch," answered the prosecutor, removing him from his knee. "Before kissing we must have a talk, and a serious talk . . . I am angry with you, and don't love you any more. I tell you, my boy, I don't love you, and you are no son of mine. . . ."

19   Seryozha looked intently at his father, then shifted his eyes to the table, and shrugged his shoulders.

20   "What have I done to you?" he asked in perplexity, blinking. "I haven't been in your study all day, and I haven't touched anything."

21   "Natalya Semyonovna has just been complaining to me that you have been smoking. . . . Is it true? Have you been smoking?"

22   "Yes, I did smoke once. . . . That's true. . . ."

23   "Now you see you are lying as well," said the prosecutor, frowning to disguise a smile. "Natalya Semyonovna has seen you smoking twice. So you see you have been detected in three misdeeds: smoking, taking someone else's tobacco, and lying. Three faults."

24   "Oh yes," Seryozha recollected, and his eyes smiled. "That's true, that's true; I smoked twice: to-day and before."

25   "So you see it was not once, but twice. . . . I am very, very much displeased with you! You used to be a good boy, but now I see you are spoilt and have become a bad one."

26   Yevgeny Petrovitch smoothed down Seryozha's collar and thought:

27   "What more am I to say to him!"

28   "Yes, it's not right," he continued. "I did not expect it of you. In the first place, you ought not to take tobacco that does not belong to you. Every person has only the right to make use of his own property; if he takes anyone else's . . . he is a bad man!" ("I am not saying the right thing!" thought Yevgeny Petrovitch.) "For instance, Natalya Semyonovna has a box with her clothes in it. That's her box, and we—that is, you and I—dare not touch it, as it is not ours. That's right,

Please note that excerpts and passages in the StudySync® library and this workbook are intended as touchstones to generate interest in an author's work. The excerpts and passages do not substitute for the reading of entire texts, and StudySync® strongly recommends that students seek out and purchase the whole literary or informational work in order to experience it as the author intended. Links to online resellers are available in our digital library. In addition, complete works may be ordered through an authorized reseller by filling out and returning to StudySync® the order form enclosed in this workbook.

Reading & Writing Companion   13

isn't it? You've got toy horses and pictures. . . . I don't take them, do I? Perhaps I might like to take them, but . . . they are not mine, but yours!"

29   "Take them if you like!" said Seryozha, raising his eyebrows. "Please don't hesitate, papa, take them! That yellow dog on your table is mine, but I don't mind. . . . Let it stay."

30   "You don't understand me," said Bykovsky. "You have given me the dog, it is mine now and I can do what I like with it; but I didn't give you the tobacco! The tobacco is mine." ("I am not explaining properly!" thought the prosecutor. "It's wrong! Quite wrong!") "If I want to smoke someone else's tobacco, I must first of all ask his permission. . . ."

31   Languidly linking one phrase on to another and imitating the language of the nursery, Bykovsky tried to explain to his son the meaning of property. Seryozha gazed at his chest and listened attentively (he liked talking to his father in the evening), then he leaned his elbow on the edge of the table and began screwing up his short-sighted eyes at the papers and the inkstand. His eyes strayed over the table and rested on the gum-bottle.

32   "Papa, what is gum made of?" he asked suddenly, putting the bottle to his eyes.

33   Bykovsky took the bottle out of his hands and set it in its place and went on:

34   "Secondly, you smoke. . . . That's very bad. Though I smoke it does not follow that you may. I smoke and know that it is stupid, I blame myself and don't like myself for it." ("A clever teacher, I am!" he thought.) "Tobacco is very bad for the health, and anyone who smokes dies earlier than he should. It's particularly bad for boys like you to smoke. Your chest is weak, you haven't reached your full strength yet, and smoking leads to **consumption** and other illness in weak people. Uncle Ignat died of consumption, you know. If he hadn't smoked, perhaps he would have lived till now."

35   Seryozha looked pensively at the lamp, touched the lamp-shade with his finger, and heaved a sigh.

36   "Uncle Ignat played the violin splendidly!" he said. "His violin is at the Grigoryevs' now."

37   Seryozha leaned his elbows on the edge of the table again, and sank into thought. His white face wore a fixed expression, as though he were listening or following a train of thought of his own; distress and something like fear came into his big staring eyes. He was most likely thinking now of death, which had so lately carried off his mother and Uncle Ignat. Death carries mothers and uncles off to the other world, while their children and violins

remain upon the earth. The dead live somewhere in the sky beside the stars, and look down from there upon the earth. Can they endure the parting?

38 "What am I to say to him?" thought Yevgeny Petrovitch. "He's not listening to me. Obviously he does not regard either his misdoings or my arguments as serious. How am I to drive it home?"

39 The prosecutor got up and walked about the study.

40 "Formerly, in my time, these questions were very simply settled," he reflected. "Every urchin who was caught smoking was thrashed. The cowardly and faint-hearted did actually give up smoking, any who were somewhat more **plucky** and intelligent, after the thrashing took to carrying tobacco in the legs of their boots, and smoking in the barn. When they were caught in the barn and thrashed again, they would go away to smoke by the river . . . and so on, till the boy grew up. My mother used to give me money and sweets not to smoke. Now that method is looked upon as worthless and immoral. The modern teacher, taking his stand on logic, tries to make the child form good principles, not from fear, nor from desire for distinction or reward, but consciously."

41 While he was walking about, thinking, Seryozha climbed up with his legs on a chair sideways to the table, and began drawing. That he might not spoil official paper nor touch the ink, a heap of half-sheets, cut on purpose for him, lay on the table together with a blue pencil.

42 "Cook was chopping up cabbage to-day and she cut her finger," he said, drawing a little house and moving his eyebrows. "She gave such a scream that we were all frightened and ran into the kitchen. Stupid thing! Natalya Semyonovna told her to dip her finger in cold water, but she sucked it . . . And how could she put a dirty finger in her mouth! That's not proper, you know, papa!"

43 Then he went on to describe how, while they were having dinner, a man with a hurdy-gurdy had come into the yard with a little girl, who had danced and sung to the music.

44 "He has his own train of thought!" thought the prosecutor. "He has a little world of his own in his head, and he has his own ideas of what is important and unimportant. To gain possession of his attention, it's not enough to imitate his language, one must also be able to think in the way he does. He would understand me perfectly if I really were sorry for the loss of the tobacco, if I felt injured and cried. . . . That's why no one can take the place of a mother in bringing up a child, because she can feel, cry, and laugh together with the child. One can do nothing by logic and morality. What more shall I say to him? What?"

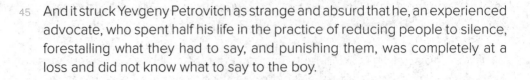

45 And it struck Yevgeny Petrovitch as strange and absurd that he, an experienced advocate, who spent half his life in the practice of reducing people to silence, forestalling what they had to say, and punishing them, was completely at a loss and did not know what to say to the boy.

46 "I say, give me your word of honour that you won't smoke again," he said.

47 "Word of hon-nour!" carolled Seryozha, pressing hard on the pencil and bending over the drawing. "Word of hon-nour!"

48 "Does he know what is meant by word of honour?" Bykovsky asked himself. "No, I am a poor teacher of morality! If some schoolmaster or one of our legal fellows could peep into my brain at this moment he would call me a poor stick, and would very likely suspect me of unnecessary subtlety. . . . But in school and in court, of course, all these wretched questions are far more simply settled than at home; here one has to do with people whom one loves beyond everything, and love is exacting and complicates the question. If this boy were not my son, but my pupil, or a prisoner on his trial, I should not be so cowardly, and my thoughts would not be racing all over the place!"

49 Yevgeny Petrovitch sat down to the table and pulled one of Seryozha's drawings to him. In it there was a house with a crooked roof, and smoke which came out of the chimney like a flash of lightning in zigzags up to the very edge of the paper; beside the house stood a soldier with dots for eyes and a bayonet that looked like the figure 4.

50 "A man can't be taller than a house," said the prosecutor.

51 Seryozha got on his knee, and moved about for some time to get comfortably settled there.

52 "No, papa!" he said, looking at his drawing. "If you were to draw the soldier small you would not see his eyes."

53 Ought he to argue with him? From daily observation of his son the prosecutor had become convinced that children, like savages, have their own artistic standpoints and requirements peculiar to them, beyond the grasp of grown-up people. Had he been attentively observed, Seryozha might have struck a grown-up person as abnormal. He thought it possible and reasonable to draw men taller than houses, and to represent in pencil, not only objects, but even his sensations. Thus he would depict the sounds of an orchestra in the form of smoke like spherical blurs, a whistle in the form of a spiral thread. . . . To his mind sound was closely connected with form and colour, so that when he painted letters he invariably painted the letter L yellow, M red, A black, and so on.

54 Abandoning his drawing, Seryozha shifted about once more, got into a comfortable attitude, and busied himself with his father's beard. First he carefully smoothed it, then he parted it and began combing it into the shape of whiskers.

55 "Now you are like Ivan Stepanovitch," he said, "and in a minute you will be like our porter. Papa, why is it porters stand by doors? Is it to prevent thieves getting in?"

56 The prosecutor felt the child's breathing on his face, he was continually touching his hair with his cheek, and there was a warm soft feeling in his soul, as soft as though not only his hands but his whole soul were lying on the velvet of Seryozha's jacket.

57 He looked at the boy's big dark eyes, and it seemed to him as though from those wide pupils there looked out at him his mother and his wife and everything that he had ever loved.

58 "To think of thrashing him . . ." he mused. "A nice task to devise a punishment for him! How can we undertake to bring up the young? In old days people were simpler and thought less, and so settled problems boldly. But we think too much, we are eaten up by logic . . . . The more developed a man is, the more he reflects and gives himself up to subtleties, the more undecided and scrupulous he becomes, and the more timidity he shows in taking action. How much courage and self-confidence it needs, when one comes to look into it closely, to undertake to teach, to judge, to write a thick book. . . ."

59 It struck ten.

60 "Come, boy, it's bedtime," said the prosecutor. "Say good-night and go."

61 "No, papa," said Seryozha, "I will stay a little longer. Tell me something! Tell me a story. . . ."

62 "Very well, only after the story you must go to bed at once."

63 Yevgeny Petrovitch on his free evenings was in the habit of telling Seryozha stories. Like most people engaged in practical affairs, he did not know a single poem by heart, and could not remember a single fairy tale, so he had to improvise. As a rule he began with the stereotyped: "In a certain country, in a certain kingdom," then he heaped up all kinds of innocent nonsense and had no notion as he told the beginning how the story would go on, and how it would end. Scenes, characters, and situations were taken at random, impromptu, and the plot and the moral came of itself as it were, with no plan on the part of the story-teller. Seryozha was very fond of this improvisation,

Please note that excerpts and passages in the StudySync® library and this workbook are intended as touchstones to generate interest in an author's work. The excerpts and passages do not substitute for the reading of entire texts, and StudySync® strongly recommends that students seek out and purchase the whole literary or informational work in order to experience it as the author intended. Links to online resellers are available in our digital library. In addition, complete works may be ordered through an authorized reseller by filling out and returning to StudySync® the order form enclosed in this workbook.

Reading & Writing
Companion   **17**

and the prosecutor noticed that the simpler and the less ingenious the plot, the stronger the impression it made on the child.

64 "Listen," he said, raising his eyes to the ceiling. "Once upon a time, in a certain country, in a certain kingdom, there lived an old, very old emperor with a long grey beard, and . . . and with great grey moustaches like this. Well, he lived in a glass palace which sparkled and glittered in the sun, like a great piece of clear ice. The palace, my boy, stood in a huge garden, in which there grew oranges, you know . . . bergamots, cherries . . . tulips, roses, and lilies-of-the-valley were in flower in it, and birds of different colours sang there. . . . Yes. . . . On the trees there hung little glass bells, and, when the wind blew, they rang so sweetly that one was never tired of hearing them. Glass gives a softer, tenderer note than metals. . . . Well, what next? There were fountains in the garden. . . . Do you remember you saw a fountain at Auntie Sonya's summer villa? Well, there were fountains just like that in the emperor's garden, only ever so much bigger, and the jets of water reached to the top of the highest poplar."

65 Yevgeny Petrovitch thought a moment, and went on:

66 "The old emperor had an only son and heir of his kingdom—a boy as little as you. He was a good boy. He was never naughty, he went to bed early, he never touched anything on the table, and altogether he was a sensible boy. He had only one fault, he used to smoke. . . ."

67 Seryozha listened attentively, and looked into his father's eyes without blinking. The prosecutor went on, thinking: "What next?" He spun out a long rigmarole, and ended like this:

68 "The emperor's son fell ill with consumption through smoking, and died when he was twenty. His infirm and sick old father was left without anyone to help him. There was no one to govern the kingdom and defend the palace. Enemies came, killed the old man, and destroyed the palace, and now there are neither cherries, nor birds, nor little bells in the garden. . . . That's what happened."

69 This ending struck Yevgeny Petrovitch as absurd and naïve, but the whole story made an intense impression on Seryozha. Again his eyes were clouded by mournfulness and something like fear; for a minute he looked pensively at the dark window, shuddered, and said, in a sinking voice:

70 "I am not going to smoke any more. . . ."

71 When he had said good-night and gone away his father walked up and down the room and smiled to himself.

72 "They would tell me it was the influence of beauty, artistic form," he meditated. "It may be so, but that's no comfort. It's not the right way, all the same. . . . Why must morality and truth never be offered in their crude form, but only with embellishments, sweetened and gilded like pills? It's not normal. . . . It's falsification . . . deception . . . tricks . . . ."

73 He thought of the jurymen to whom it was absolutely necessary to make a "speech," of the general public who absorb history only from legends and historical novels, and of himself and how he had gathered an understanding of life not from sermons and laws, but from fables, novels, poems.

74 "Medicine should be sweet, truth beautiful, and man has had this foolish habit since the days of Adam . . . though, indeed, perhaps it is all natural, and ought to be so. . . . There are many deceptions and delusions in nature that serve a purpose."

75 He set to work, but lazy, intimate thoughts still strayed through his mind for a good while. Overhead the scales could no longer be heard, but the inhabitant of the second storey was still pacing from one end of the room to another.

 THINK QUESTIONS   CA-CCSS: CA.RL.8.1, CA.RL.8.3, CA.RL.8.4, CA.L.8.4a, CA.L.8.4d

1. What problem does Yevgeny have at the beginning of the story, and why does he find it so difficult to solve? Cite textual evidence to support your answer.

2. What line of reasoning does Yevgeny first use with his son about taking his tobacco, and why does it not get through to Seryozha? Cite textual evidence to support your answer.

3. How does Yevgeny finally get through to Seryozha, getting a promise from his son that he will no longer smoke? Support your answer with textual evidence.

4. Use context to determine the meaning of the word **discursive** as it is used in "Home." Write your definition of "discursive" and tell how you found it.

5. Use the synonyms and antonyms provided in the passage to determine the meaning of plucky as it is used in "Home." Write your definition of **"plucky"** and tell how you got it.

CLOSE READ   CA-CCSS: CA.RL.8.1, CA.RL.8.3, CA.RL.8.4, CA.W.8.2

Reread the short story "Home." As you reread, complete the Focus Questions below. Then use your answers and annotations from the questions to help you complete the Writing Prompt

FOCUS QUESTIONS

1. Reread the eighth and ninth paragraphs of the story. Why does Yevgeny have conflicting feelings about the idea of punishing someone for smoking? Highlight textual evidence from the story to support your answer.

2. How does Chekhov use interior monologue to show the changes Yevgeny goes through as he tries to think of ways to discipline his son? Highlight textual evidence from the story to explain your answer.

3. Why does Yevgeny become frustrated after attempting to reason logically with his son? Highlight evidence from the text and make annotations to support your explanation.

4. In the eleventh paragraph, Chekhov mentions the pacing of a man overhead who, to judge from his nervous step, was "thinking of something harassing." At the end of the story, after Yevgeny has sent Seryozha to bed, the author mentions that "the inhabitant of the second storey was still pacing from one end of the room to another." In what way do the actions of this unnamed, secondary character reflect Yevgeny's state of mind in the story? Highlight evidence from the text to support your answer.

5. Think about the title Chekhov has given this short story. In light of Yevgeny's profession, what takes place in the story, and what Yevgeny learns about how to get through to his son, why is the title "Home" so appropriate? Support your answer with textual evidence

WRITING PROMPT

Yevgeny Petrovitch Bykovsky states that he achieves an understanding of life from sermons and laws, not from fables, novels, and poems. How does he change throughout the story? Write an essay of least 300 words explaining how he moves from logic to the use of stories and fairy tales as he attempts to reason with his son. Use textual evidence from the story to support your ideas.

A CELEBRATION OF GRANDFATHERS

NON-FICTION
Rudolfo Anaya
1983

INTRODUCTION

As a young man, Rudolfo Anaya loved to read, but he could not find books that reflected his own Mexican American history and culture. Today, Anaya is a well-known writer who has published novels, short stories, plays, poems, and children's books that have contributed to the growing body of Chicano literature. In this essay, Anaya reflects on the life lessons he learned from his grandfather.

"They learned that to survive one had to share in the process of life."

 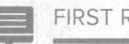

NOTES

FIRST READ

1 "Buenos Dias le de Dios, abuelo." God give you a good day, grandfather. This is how I was taught as a child to greet my grandfather, or any grown person. It was a greeting of respect, a cultural value to be passed on from generation to generation, this respect for the old ones.

2 The old people I remember from my childhood were strong in their beliefs, and as we lived daily with them we learned a wise path of life to follow. They had something important to share with the young, and when they spoke the young listened. These old abuelos and abuelitas had worked the earth all their lives, and so they knew the value of nurturing, they knew the sensitivity of the earth. The daily struggle called for cooperation, and so every person contributed to the social fabric, and each person was respected for his contribution.

3 The old ones had looked deep into the web that connects all animate and **inanimate** forms of life, and they recognized the great design of creation.

4 These ancianos from the cultures of the Rio Grande, lived side by side, sharing, growing together, they knew the rhythms and cycles of time, from the preparation of the earth in the spring to the digging of the acequias that bought the water to the dance of harvest in the fall. They shared good times and hard times. They helped each other through epidemics and the personal tragedies, they shared what little they had when the winds burned the land and no rain came. They learned that to survive one had to share in the process of life.

5 Hard workers all, they tilled the earth and farmed, ran the herds and spun wool, and carved their saints and their kachinas from cottonwood late in the winter nights. All worked with a deep faith which perplexes the modern mind.

NOTES

6   Their faith shone in their eyes; it was in the strength of their grip, in the creases time wove into their faces. When they spoke, they spoke plainly and with few words, and they meant what they said. When they prayed, they went straight to the source of life. When there were good times, they knew how to dance in celebrations and how to prepare the foods of the fiestas. All this they passed on to the young, so that a new generation would know what they had known, so the string of life would not be broken.

7   Today we would say that the old abuelitos lived **authentic** lives.

8   Newcomers to New Mexico often say that time seems to move slowly here. I think they mean that they have come in contact with the inner strength of the people, a strength so solid it causes time itself to pause. Think of it. Think of the high northern New Mexico villages, or the lonely ranches on the open llano. Think of the Indian **pueblo** which lies as solid as rock in the face of time. Remember the old people whose eyes seem like windows that peer into the distant past that makes absurdity of our contemporary world. That is what one feels when one encounters the old ones and their land, a pausing of time.

9   We have all felt time stand still. We have all been in the presence of power, the knowledge of the old ones, the majestic peace of a mountain stream or an aspen grove or red buttes rising into blue sky. We have all felt the light of dusk permeate the earth and cause time to pause in its flow.

10 I felt this when I first touched the spirit of Ultima, the old curandera who appears in my first novel, Bless Me, Ultima.This is how the young Antonio describes what he feels:

11 When she came the beauty of the llano unfolded before my eyes, and the gurgling waters of the river sang to the hum of the turning earth. The magical time of childhood stood still, and the pulse of the living earth pressed its mystery into my living blood. She took my hand, and the silent, magical powers she possessed made beauty from the raw, sun-baked llano, the green river valley, and the blue bowl which was the white sun's home. My bare feet felt the throbbing earth, and my body trembled with excitement. Time stood still...

12 At other times, in other places, when I have been privileged to be with the old ones, to learn, I have felt this inner reserve of strength from which they draw. I have been held motionless and speechless by the power of curanderas. I have felt the same power when I hunted with Cruz, high on the Taos Mountain, where it was more than the incredible beauty of the mountain bathed in morning light, more that the shining of the quivering aspen, but a connection with life, as if a shining strand of light connected the particular and the cosmic. That feeling is an epiphany of time, a standing still of time.

13 But not all of our old ones are curanderos or hunters on the mountain. My grandfather was a plain man, a fan from the valley called Puerto de Luna on Pecos River. He was probably a descendant of those people who spilled over the mountain from Taos, following the Pecos River in search of farmland. There in that river valley he settled and raised a large family.

14 Bearded and walrus-mustached, he stood five feet tall, but to me as a child he was a giant. I remember him most for his silence. In the summers my parents sent me to live with him on his farm, for I was to learn the ways of a farmer. My uncles also lived in that valley, there where only the flow of the river and the whispering of the wind marked time. For me it was a magical place.

15 I remember once, while out in the fields, I came upon an anthill, and before I knew it I was badly bitten. After he had covered my welts with the cool mud from the irrigation ditch, my grandfather calmly said: "Know where you stand." That is the way he spoke, in short phrases, to the point.

16 One very dry summer, the river dried to a trickle, there was no water for the fields. The young plants withered and died. In my sadness and with the impulse of youth I said, "I wish it would rain!" My grandfather touched me, looked up into the sky and whispered, "Pray for rain." In his language there was a difference. He felt connected to the cycles that brought the rain or kept it from us. His prayer was a meaningful action, because he was a participant with the forces that filled our world, he was not a **bystander**.

17 A young man died at the village one summer. A very tragic death. He was dragged by his horse. When he was found I cried, for the boy was my friend. I did not understand why death had come to one so young. My grandfather took me aside and said: "Think of the death of the trees and the fields in the fall. The leaves fall, and everything rests, as if dead. But they bloom again in the spring. Death is only this small transformation in life."

18 These are the things I remember, these fleeting images, few words.

19 I remember him driving his horse-drawn wagon into Santa Rosa in the fall when he brought his harvest produce to sell in the town. What a tower of strength seemed to come in that small man huddled on the seat of the giant wagon. One click of his tongue and the horses obeyed, stopped or turned as he wished. He never raised his whip. How unlike today when so much teaching is done with loud words and threatening hands.

20 I would run to greet the wagon, and the wagon would stop. "Buenos Dias le de Dios, abuelo," I would say. "Buenos Dias te de Dios, mi hijo," he would answer and smile, and then I could jump up on the wagon and sit at his side. Then I, too, became a king as I rode next to the old man who smelled of earth

NOTES

and sweat and the other deep aromas from the orchards and fields of Puerto de Luna.

21 We were all sons and daughters to him. But today the sons and daughters are breaking with the past, putting aside los abuelitos.' The old values are threatened, and threatened most where it comes to these relationships with the old people. If we don't take the time to watch and feel the years of their final transformation, a part of our humanity will be lessened.

22 I grew up speaking Spanish, and oh! how difficult it was to learn English. Sometimes I give up and cry out that I couldn't learn. Then he would say, "Ten paciencia." Have patience. Paciencia, a word with the strength of centuries, a word that said that someday we would overcome. Paciencia, how soothing a word coming from this old man who could still sling hundred-pound bags over his shoulder, chop wood for hundreds of hours on end, and hitch up his own horses and ride to town and back in one day.

23 "You have to learn the language of the Americanos," he said. "Me, I will live my last days in my valley. You will live in a new time, the time of the gringos."

24 A new time did come, a new time is here. How will we form it so it is fruitful? We need to know where we stand. We need to speak softly and respect others, and to share what we have. We need to pray not for material gain, but for rain for the fields, for the sun to nurture growth, for nights in which we can sleep in peace, and for a harvest in which everyone can share. Simple lessons from a simple man. These lessons he learned from his past, which was as deep and strong as the currents of the river of life, a life which could be stronger than death.

25 He was a man; he died. Not in his valley, but nevertheless cared for by his sons and daughters and flocks of grandchildren. At the end, I would enter his room, which carried the smell of medications and Vicks. Gone were the aromas of the fields, the strength of his young manhood. Gone also was his patience in the face of crippling old age. Small things bothered him; he shouted or turned sour when his expectations were not met. It was because he could not care for himself, because he was returning to that state of childhood, and all those wishes and desires were now wrapped in a crumbling old body.

26 "Ten paciencia," I once said to him, and he smiled. "I didn't know I would grow this old," he said.

27 I would sit and look at him and remember what was said of him when he was a young man. He could mount a wild horse and break it, and he could ride as far as any man. He could dance all night at a dance, then work the acequia

Copyright © BookheadEd Learning, LLC

NOTES

the following day. He helped the neighbors, they helped him. He married, raised children. Small legends, the kind that make up every man's life.

28   He was ninety-four when he died. Family, neighbors, and friends gathered; they all agreed he had led a rich life. I remembered the last years, the years he spent in bed. And as I remember now, I am reminded that it is too easy to romanticize old age. Sometimes we forget the pain of the transformation into old age, we forget the natural breaking down of the body. Not all go gentle into the last years, some go crying and cursing, forgetting the names of those they love the most, withdrawing into an internal anguish few of us can know. May we be granted the patience and care to deal with our ancianos.

29   For some time we haven't looked at these changes and needs of the old ones. The American image created by the mass media is an image of youth, not of old age. It is the beautiful and the young who are praised in this society. If analyzed carefully, we see that same damaging thought has crept into the way society views the old. In response to the old, the mass media have just created old people who act like the young. It is only the healthy, pink-cheeked, outgoing, older persons we are shown in the media. And they are always selling something, as if an entire generation of old people were salesmen in their lives. Commercials show very lively old men, who must always be in excellent health according to the new myth, selling insurance policies or real estate as they are out golfing; older women selling coffee or toilet paper to those just married. That image does not illustrate the real life of old ones.

30   Real life takes into account the natural cycle of growth and change. My grandfather pointed to the leaves falling from the tree. So time brings with its transformation the often painful, wearing-down process. Vision blurs, health wanes even the act of walking carries with it the painful reminder of the autumn of life. But this process is something to be faced, not something to be hidden away by false images. Yes, the old can be young at heart, but in their own way, with their own dignity. They do not have to copy the always-young image of the Hollywood star.

31   My grandfather wanted to return to his valley to die. But by then the families of the valley had left in search of a better future. It is only now that there seems to be a return to the valley, a revival. The new generation seeks its roots, that value of love for the land moves us to return to the place where our ancianos formed the culture.

32   I returned to Puerto de Luna last summer, to join the community in a celebration of the founding of the church. I drove by my grandfather's home, my uncles' ranches, the neglected **adobe** washing down into the earth from whence it came. And I wondered, how might the values of my grandfather's generation live in our own? What can we retain to see us through these hard times? I was

NOTES

to become a farmer, and I became a writer. As I plow and plant my words, do I nurture as my grandfather did in his fields and orchards? The answers are not simple.

33 "They don't make men like that anymore," is a phrase we hear when one does honor to a man. I am glad I knew my grandfather. I am glad there are still times when I can see him in my dreams, hear him in my reverie. Sometimes I think I catch a whiff of that earthy aroma that was his smell. Then I smile. How strong these people were to leave such a lasting impression.

34 So, as I would greet my abuelo long ago, it would help us all to greet the old ones we know with this kind and respectful greeting: "Buenos Dias le de Dios."

From "A Celebration of Grandfathers." Copyright © 1983 by Rudolfo Anaya. First published in NEW MEXICO MAGAZINE, March 1983. By permission of Susan Bergholz Literary Services, New York, NY and Lamy, NM. All rights reserved.

THINK QUESTIONS   CA-CCSS: CA.RI.8.1, CA.L.8.4a, CA.L.8.4b

1. Who are the *ancianos*? Write two or three sentences describing the different ways the author remembers them. Use textual evidence to explain your answer.

2. What does the author say about the importance of "sharing" among the old ones? Use textual evidence to explain your answer.

3. What is Anaya's memory of his grandfather's size? Why is this important? Provide textual evidence to describe how the grandfather looked and acted, as the author remembers him.

4. The Spanish word *pueblo* comes from the Latin root *populus*, meaning "people." Use this information as well as context clues to determine the meaning of **pueblo** as it is used in "A Celebration of Grandfathers." Write your definition of "*pueblo*" and tell how you found it.

5. The Spanish word **adobe** often appears in English. Use context clues to determine the meaning of "*adobe*." Write your definition of "*adobe*" and tell how you got it.

Please note that excerpts and passages in the StudySync® library and this workbook are intended as touchstones to generate interest in an author's work. The excerpts and passages do not substitute for the reading of entire texts, and StudySync® strongly recommends that students seek out and purchase the whole literary or informational work in order to experience it as the author intended. Links to online resellers are available in our digital library. In addition, complete works may be ordered through an authorized reseller by filling out and returning to StudySync® the order form enclosed in this workbook.

Reading & Writing Companion   **27**

CLOSE READ
CA-CCSS: CA.RI.8.1, CA.RI.8.2, CA.RI.8.6, CA.W.8.4, CA.W.8.5, CA.W.8.6, CA.W.8.10

Reread the essay "A Celebration of Grandfathers." As you reread, complete the Focus Questions below. Then use your answers and annotations from the questions to help you complete the Writing Prompt.

FOCUS QUESTIONS

1. In paragraph 4, the author says that the old people "shared good times and hard times." How is the concept of *sharing* key to understanding the central idea of this essay? Highlight evidence from the text and make annotations to explain your choices. In your annotations, explain how *sharing* relates both to the old people Anaya discusses and to readers today.

2. In paragraph 8, Anaya talks about the concept of time. How does Anaya describe time, and how does this relate to other ideas in the essay? Highlight textual evidence and make annotations to support your explanation.

3. Review paragraph 22, which begins, "I grew up speaking Spanish....". The author emphasizes his grandfather's physical abilities, but he also discusses his mental abilities. What is the main idea of this paragraph, and how do the details support it? Highlight textual evidence and make annotations to explain your choices.

4. Review paragraph 32, which begins, "I returned to Puerto de Luna...". Here, the author offers a summary of what he has been discussing. What does this summary help emphasize about the essay? Finally, what is the essay's central or main idea? Highlight evidence from the text and make annotations to support your explanation.

5. How do you think the author would answer the Essential Question of this unit: "How can life experiences shape our values?" Keep in mind what the author has stressed as the central or main idea, as well as the details he has used to support it. Highlight evidence from the text and make annotations to support your explanation.

WRITING PROMPT

How does the central or main idea that the author has advanced in "A Celebration of Grandfathers" help you understand the author's purpose for writing this essay? How does his use of personal memories help to make his purpose clear? Use your understanding of supporting details and ideas to explain how the author builds up a central or main idea in the essay. Support your writing with evidence from the text.

MOTHER TO SON

POETRY
Langston Hughes
1922

INTRODUCTION

African-American poet Langston Hughes is a one of the best-known poets of the Harlem Renaissance, a cultural and intellectual movement that began in the 1920s and resulted in the production of African-American literature, art, and music that challenged racism and promoted progressive politics, such as racial and social integration. In Hughes' poem "Mother to Son," the speaker is a mother who draws on her own experiences to teach her son about perseverance.

"Life for me ain't been no crystal stair."

 FIRST READ

1 Well, son, I'll tell you:
2 Life for me ain't been no **crystal** stair.
3 It's had tacks in it,
4 And **splinters,**
5 And boards torn up,
6 And places with no carpet on the floor—
7 Bare.
8 But all the time.
9 I'se been a-climbin' on,
10 And reachin' **landin's,**
11 And turnin' corners,
12 And sometimes goin' in the dark
13 Where there ain't been no light.
14 So, boy, don't you turn back.
15 Don't you set down on the steps
16 'Cause you finds it's kinder hard.
17 Don't you fall now—
18 For I'se still goin', honey,
19 I'se still climbin',
20 And life for me ain't been no crystal stair.

THINK QUESTIONS   CA-CCSS: CA.RL.8.1, CA.L.8.4a, CA.L.8.5a

1. What does the poem's speaker mean when she says that her life "ain't been no crystal stair"? Which details in lines 1–7 of the poem explain her meaning, as well as who she is?

2. How does the poet continue using the image of the staircase in lines 8–13? What do you think the mother means by these images? Use textual evidence to support your answer.

3. Refer to lines 15–20 to summarize the mother's advice to her son. Support your answer with textual evidence.

4. Use context clues to determine the meaning of the figure of speech **crystal** stair as it is used in "Mother to Son." Write your definition of *"crystal" stair* and tell how you got it.

5. Use context clues in the poem to determine the meaning of **splinters**. Write your definition of *splinters* and tell how you got it.

Please note that excerpts and passages in the StudySync® library and this workbook are intended as touchstones to generate interest in an author's work. The excerpts and passages do not substitute for the reading of entire texts, and StudySync® strongly recommends that students seek out and purchase the whole literary or informational work in order to experience it as the author intended. Links to online resellers are available in our digital library. In addition, complete works may be ordered through an authorized reseller by filling out and returning to StudySync® the order form enclosed in this workbook.

Reading & Writing Companion   **31**

CLOSE READ

CA-CCSS: CA.RL.8.1, CA.RL.8.2, CA.RL.8.3, CA.RL.8.4, CA.W.8.2

Reread the poem "Mother to Son." As you reread, complete the Focus Questions below. Then use your answers and annotations from the questions to help you complete the Writing Prompt.

FOCUS QUESTIONS

1. The mother begins by saying, "Well, son, I'll tell you: / Life for me ain't been no crystal stair." What kind of a life might be described as a "crystal stair"? How is this kind of stair different from the mother's "stair"? Highlight your textual evidence and make annotations to explain your inferences, noting how the descriptions affect the poem's tone.

2. Lines 3–7 describe the wooden staircase that is the metaphor or image for the mother's life. What might the "tacks," "splinters," and "boards torn up" in the staircase represent? What could the "Bare" places stand for? Finally, what do these details reveal about the poem's speaker? Highlight these details in the poem. Use them as textual evidence for the annotations that you make to explain what each of these represents.

3. Why is the mother so proud of "a-climbin' on," "reachin' landin's," and "turnin' corners"? What might this figurative language refer to? Highlight these details in the poem. Use them as textual evidence for the annotations that you make to explain what each of these phrases might represent.

4. What actions in life might the mother be referring to when she tells her son, "Don't you turn back. / Don't you set down on the steps / 'Cause you finds it's kinder hard. / Don't you fall now—"? What might have caused the mother to give this advice to her son? Highlight the advice she gives. Then make annotations to explain your inferences about the son's life.

5. Think about the poem as a whole. How does the mother's figurative language help readers understand the poem's tone, or the author's attitude toward the woman and her values? Highlight textual evidence and make annotations to explain your answer. Finally, state the poem's theme or meaning.

Copyright © BookheadEd Learning, LLC

WRITING PROMPT

Write an objective summary of the poem "Mother to Son," including its theme or message. Explain how the author creates a specific tone using figurative language and dialect to convey this message. Then compare and contrast the poem with the structure and theme of another text you have read in this unit, such as "Home" or "Abuela Invents the Zero." Analyze how the differing structure of each text contributes to its meaning and style. Support your writing with evidence from both texts.

LITTLE WOMEN

FICTION
Louisa May Alcott
1869

INTRODUCTION

Louisa May Alcott (1832–1888) is one of America's most beloved and popular authors. Originally published in two volumes, *Little Women* follows the lives of the four March sisters—Meg, Jo, Beth, and Amy—as they grow up lacking money but not love in Civil War-era New England. In this excerpt, the girls prepare to surprise their mother at Christmas and, in the process, learn something about the spirit of giving.

"That was a very happy breakfast, though they didn't get any of it."

NOTES

 FIRST READ

From Chapter 1: "Playing Pilgrims"

1   The clock struck six and, having swept up the **hearth**, Beth put a pair of slippers down to warm. Somehow the sight of the old shoes had a good effect upon the girls, for Mother was coming, and everyone brightened to welcome her. Meg stopped lecturing, and lighted the lamp, Amy got out of the easy chair without being asked, and Jo forgot how tired she was as she sat up to hold the slippers nearer to the blaze.

2   "They are quite worn out. Marmee must have a new pair."

3   "I thought I'd get her some with my dollar," said Beth.

4   "No, I shall!" cried Amy.

5   "I'm the oldest," began Meg, but Jo cut in with a decided, "I'm the man of the family now Papa is away, and I shall provide the slippers, for he told me to take special care of Mother while he was gone."

6   "I'll tell you what we'll do," said Beth, "let's each get her something for Christmas, and not get anything for ourselves."

7   "That's like you, dear! What will we get?" exclaimed Jo.

8   Everyone thought soberly for a minute, then Meg announced, as if the idea was suggested by the sight of her own pretty hands, "I shall give her a nice pair of gloves."

9   "Army shoes, best to be had," cried Jo.

10   "Some handkerchiefs, all hemmed," said Beth.

Copyright © BookheadEd Learning, LLC

NOTES

11 "I'll get a little bottle of cologne. She likes it, and it won't cost much, so I'll have some left to buy my pencils," added Amy.

12 "How will we give the things?" asked Meg.

13 "Put them on the table, and bring her in and see her open the bundles. Don't you remember how we used to do on our birthdays?" answered Jo.

14 "I used to be so frightened when it was my turn to sit in the chair with the crown on, and see you all come marching round to give the presents, with a kiss. I liked the things and the kisses, but it was dreadful to have you sit looking at me while I opened the bundles," said Beth, who was toasting her face and the bread for tea at the same time.

15 "Let Marmee think we are getting things for ourselves, and then surprise her. We must go shopping tomorrow afternoon, Meg. There is so much to do about the play for Christmas night," said Jo, marching up and down, with her hands behind her back, and her nose in the air.

· · ·

From Chapter 2: "A Merry Christmas"

16 "Where is Mother?" asked Meg, as she and Jo ran down to thank her for their gifts, half an hour later.

17 "Goodness only knows. Some poor creeter came a-beggin', and your ma went straight off to see what was needed. There never was such a woman for givin' away vittlesand drink, clothes and firin'," replied Hannah, who had lived with the family since Meg was born, and was considered by them all more as a friend than a servant.

18 "She will be back soon, I think, so fry your cakes, and have everything ready," said Meg, looking over the presents which were collected in a basket and kept under the sofa, ready to be produced at the proper time. "Why, where is Amy's bottle of cologne?" she added, as the little flask did not appear.

19 "She took it out a minute ago, and went off with it to put a ribbon on it, or some such notion," replied Jo, dancing about the room to take the first stiffness off the new army slippers.

20 "How nice my handkerchiefs look, don't they? Hannah washed and ironed them for me, and I marked them all myself," said Beth, looking proudly at the somewhat uneven letters which had cost her such labor.

21   "Bless the child! She's gone and put 'Mother' on them instead of 'M. March'. How funny!" cried Jo, taking one up.

22   "Isn't that right? I thought it was better to do it so, because Meg's initials are M.M., and I don't want anyone to use these but Marmee," said Beth, looking troubled.

23   "It's all right, dear, and a very pretty idea, quite sensible too, for no one can ever mistake now. It will please her very much, I know," said Meg, with a frown for Jo and a smile for Beth.

24   "There's Mother. Hide the basket, quick!" cried Jo, as a door slammed and steps sounded in the hall.

25   Amy came in hastily, and looked rather **abashed** when she saw her sisters all waiting for her.

26   "Where have you been, and what are you hiding behind you?" asked Meg, surprised to see, by her hood and cloak, that lazy Amy had been out so early.

27   "Don't laugh at me, Jo! I didn't mean anyone should know till the time came. I only meant to change the little bottle for a big one, and I gave all my money to get it, and I'm truly trying not to be selfish any more."

28   As she spoke, Amy showed the handsome flask which replaced the cheap one, and looked so earnest and humble in her little effort to forget herself that Meg hugged her on the spot, and Jo pronounced her 'a trump', while Beth ran to the window, and picked her finest rose to ornament the **stately** bottle.

29   "You see I felt ashamed of my present, after reading and talking about being good this morning, so I ran round the corner and changed it the minute I was up, and I'm so glad, for mine is the handsomest now."

30   Another bang of the street door sent the basket under the sofa, and the girls to the table, eager for breakfast.

31   "Merry Christmas, Marmee! Many of them! Thank you for our books. We read some, and mean to every day," they all cried in chorus.

32   "Merry Christmas, little daughters! I'm glad you began at once, and hope you will keep on. But I want to say one word before we sit down. Not far away from here lies a poor woman with a little newborn baby. Six children are huddled into one bed to keep from freezing, for they have no fire. There is nothing to eat over there, and the oldest boy came to tell me they were suffering hunger and cold. My girls, will you give them your breakfast as a Christmas present?"

Copyright © BookheadEd Learning, LLC

33 They were all unusually hungry, having waited nearly an hour, and for a minute no one spoke, only a minute, for Jo exclaimed impetuously, "I'm so glad you came before we began!"

34 "May I go and help carry the things to the poor little children?" asked Beth eagerly.

35 "I shall take the cream and the muffins," added Amy, heroically giving up the article she most liked.

36 Meg was already covering the buckwheats, and piling the bread into one big plate.

37 "I thought you'd do it," said Mrs. March, smiling as if satisfied. "You shall all go and help me, and when we come back we will have bread and milk for breakfast, and make it up at dinnertime."

38 They were soon ready, and the procession set out. Fortunately it was early, and they went through back streets, so few people saw them, and no one laughed at the queer party.

39 A poor, bare, miserable room it was, with broken windows, no fire, ragged bedclothes, a sick mother, wailing baby, and a group of pale, hungry children cuddled under one old quilt, trying to keep warm.

40 How the big eyes stared and the blue lips smiled as the girls went in.

41 "Ach, mein Gott! It is good angels come to us!" said the poor woman, crying for joy.

42 "Funny angels in hoods and mittens," said Jo, and set them to laughing.

43 In a few minutes it really did seem as if kind spirits had been at work there. Hannah, who had carried wood, made a fire, and stopped up the broken panes with old hats and her own cloak. Mrs. March gave the mother tea and **gruel**, and comforted her with promises of help, while she dressed the little baby as tenderly as if it had been her own. The girls meantime spread the table, set the children round the fire, and fed them like so many hungry birds, laughing, talking, and trying to understand the funny broken English.

44 "Das ist gut!" "Die Engel-kinder!" cried the poor things as they ate and warmed their purple hands at the comfortable blaze. The girls had never been called angel children before, and thought it very agreeable, especially Jo, who had been considered a 'Sancho' ever since she was born. That was a very happy breakfast, though they didn't get any of it. And when they went away, leaving comfort behind, I think there were not in all the city four merrier people than

 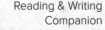

the hungry little girls who gave away their breakfasts and contented themselves with bread and milk on Christmas morning.

45 "That's loving our neighbor better than ourselves, and I like it," said Meg, as they set out their presents while their mother was upstairs collecting clothes for the poor Hummels.

 **THINK QUESTIONS** CA-CCSS: CA.RL.8.1, CA.RL.8.4, CA.L.8.4a, CA.L.8.4c, CA.L.8.4d, CA.SL.8.1a, CA.SL.8.1c, CA.SL.8.1d, CA.SL.8.4

1. Which of the four March sisters seems to be the most "in charge," or confident? Which of them seems to be more hesitant, and unsure of herself? Use textual evidence from Chapter 1 to support your answer.

2. What kind of relationship do the four March daughters seem to have with their mother? Support your answer with evidence from the text.

3. What textual clues does the author provide to indicate that the people in need on Christmas morning are an immigrant family?

4. Use context to determine the meaning of the word **abashed** as it is used in Chapter 2. Write your definition of the word, and tell how you figured it out.

5. Use context to determine the meaning of the word vittles as it is used in Chapter 2 of "Little Women." Write your definition of **"vittles"** and explain how you found it. Consult a dictionary or other resource to check the pronunciation as well as the word's etymology, or origin. In addition, verify the meaning you determined using context.

CLOSE READ
CA-CCSS: CA.RL.8.1, CA.RL.8.2, CA.RL.8.3, CA.W.8.4, CA.W.8.5, CA.W.8.6, CA.W.8.10

Reread the excerpt from *Little Women.* As you reread, complete the Focus Questions below. Then use your answers and annotations from the questions to help you complete the Writing Prompt.

FOCUS QUESTIONS

1. How does Louisa May Alcott use dialogue rather than description to reveal aspects, or character traits, of each of the March sisters? Highlight evidence in the text and make annotations to support your answer.

2. What does Amy's sudden decision to exchange the original gift she bought for Marmee reveal about her character? Highlight and label evidence in Chapter 2 to support your answer.

3. How does Marmee provoke a decision from her daughters by asking them if they will help a needy family, instead of simply telling them to do so? Highlight evidence to support your answer.

4. How is the theme of sacrifice for the greater good developed over the course of these two chapters in *Little Women?* Highlight evidence from the text to support your answer.

5. How does an experience with a needy immigrant family help shape the values of the March sisters? Highlight and annotate evidence to support your answer.

WRITING PROMPT

In this excerpt from *Little Women,* how do the similarities and differences of the four March sisters help propel the plot? Explain the similarities and differences between each of these characters, and then explain how they affect the events of the plot. Use dialogue and other details from the text to support your statements about both the characters and the plot events.

Please note that excerpts and passages in the StudySync® library and this workbook are intended as touchstones to generate interest in an author's work. The excerpts and passages do not substitute for the reading of entire texts, and StudySync® strongly recommends that students seek out and purchase the whole literary or informational work in order to experience it as the author intended. Links to online resellers are available in our digital library. In addition, complete works may be ordered through an authorized reseller by filling out and returning to StudySync® the order form enclosed in this workbook.

Reading & Writing Companion   **39**

THE ADVENTURES OF TOM SAWYER
(CHAPTER 2)

FICTION

Mark Twain
1876

INTRODUCTION

Humorously written by Mark Twain in the colorful vernacular found in the mid-19th Century along the Mississippi, *The Adventures of Tom Sawyer* is the coming of age story of one of America's great fictional characters. On a beautiful Saturday morning when he'd rather be down by the river with his friends, Tom Sawyer's Aunt Polly has given him a dreary task: whitewashing the front fence, thirty yards long and nine feet high. The charismatic Tom must use his sharp wit to try to get someone to do his work for him. But how? In this excerpt, Mark Twain's endearing character returns to the whitewashing determined to leverage all he knows about human nature to free himself of his chore.

"At this dark and hopeless moment an inspiration burst upon him!"

FIRST READ

1   He began to think of the fun he had planned for this day, and his sorrows multiplied. Soon the free boys would come tripping along on all sorts of delicious expeditions, and they would make a world of fun of him for having to work—the very thought of it burnt him like fire. He got out his worldly wealth and examined it—bits of toys, marbles, and trash; enough to buy an exchange of WORK, maybe, but not half enough to buy so much as half an hour of pure freedom. So he returned his straitened means to his pocket, and gave up the idea of trying to buy the boys. At this dark and hopeless moment an inspiration burst upon him! Nothing less than a great, magnificent inspiration.

2   He took up his brush and went tranquilly to work. Ben Rogers hove in sight presently—the very boy, of all boys, whose ridicule he had been dreading. Ben's gait was the hop-skip-and-jump—proof enough that his heart was light and his anticipations high. He was eating an apple, and giving a long, melodious whoop, at intervals, followed by a deep-toned ding-dong-dong, ding-dong-dong, for he was personating a steamboat. As he drew near, he slackened speed, took the middle of the street, leaned far over to **starboard** and rounded to ponderously and with laborious pomp and circumstance—for he was personating the Big Missouri, and considered himself to be drawing nine feet of water. He was boat and captain and engine-bells combined, so he had to imagine himself standing on his own hurricane-deck giving the orders and executing them:

3   "Stop her, sir! Ting-a-ling-ling!" The headway ran almost out, and he drew up slowly toward the sidewalk.

4   "Ship up to back! Ting-a-ling-ling!" His arms straightened and stiffened down his sides.

5   "Set her back on the stabboard! Ting-a-ling-ling! Chow! ch-chow-wow! Chow!" His right hand, mean-time, describing stately circles—for it was representing a forty-foot wheel....

6   Tom went on whitewashing—paid no attention to the steamboat. Ben stared a moment and then said: "Hi-YI! YOU'RE up a stump, ain't you!"

7   No answer. Tom surveyed his last touch with the eye of an artist, then he gave his brush another gentle sweep and surveyed the result, as before. Ben ranged up alongside of him. Tom's mouth watered for the apple, but he stuck to his work. Ben said:

8   "Hello, old chap, you got to work, hey?"

9   Tom wheeled suddenly and said:

10   "Why, it's you, Ben! I warn't noticing."

11   "Say—I'm going in a-swimming, I am. Don't you wish you could? But of course you'd druther WORK—wouldn't you? Course you would!"

12   Tom contemplated the boy a bit, and said:

13   "What do you call work?"

14   "Why, ain't THAT work?"

15   Tom resumed his whitewashing, and answered carelessly:

16   "Well, maybe it is, and maybe it ain't. All I know, is, it suits Tom Sawyer."

17   "Oh come, now, you don't mean to let on that you LIKE it?"

18   The brush continued to move.

19   "Like it? Well, I don't see why I oughtn't to like it. Does a boy get a chance to whitewash a fence every day?"

20   That put the thing in a new light. Ben stopped nibbling his apple. Tom swept his brush daintily back and forth—stepped back to note the effect—added a touch here and there—criticised the effect again—Ben watching every move and getting more and more interested, more and more absorbed. Presently he said:

21   "Say, Tom, let ME whitewash a little."

22   Tom considered, was about to consent; but he altered his mind:

23   "No—no—I reckon it wouldn't hardly do, Ben. You see, Aunt Polly's awful particular about this fence—right here on the street, you know—but if it was the back fence I wouldn't mind and SHE wouldn't. Yes, she's awful particular about this fence; it's got to be done very careful; I reckon there ain't one boy in a thousand, maybe two thousand, that can do it the way it's got to be done."

24   "No—is that so? Oh come, now—lemme just try. Only just a little—I'd let YOU, if you was me, Tom."

25   "Ben, I'd like to, honest injun; but Aunt Polly—well, Jim wanted to do it, but she wouldn't let him; Sid wanted to do it, and she wouldn't let Sid. Now don't you see how I'm fixed? If you was to tackle this fence and anything was to happen to it—"

26   "Oh, shucks, I'll be just as careful. Now lemme try. Say—I'll give you the core of my apple."

27   "Well, here—No, Ben, now don't. I'm afeard—"

28   "I'll give you ALL of it!"

29   Tom gave up the brush with reluctance in his face, but **alacrity** in his heart. And while the late steamer Big Missouri worked and sweated in the sun, the retired artist sat on a barrel in the shade close by, dangled his legs, munched his apple, and planned the slaughter of more innocents. There was no lack of material; boys happened along every little while; they came to jeer, but remained to whitewash. By the time Ben was fagged out, Tom had traded the next chance to Billy Fisher for a kite, in good repair; and when he played out, Johnny Miller bought in for a dead rat and a string to swing it with—and so on, and so on, hour after hour. And when the middle of the afternoon came, from being a poor poverty-stricken boy in the morning, Tom was literally rolling in wealth. He had besides the things before mentioned, twelve marbles, part of a jews-harp, a piece of blue bottle-glass to look through, a spool cannon, a key that wouldn't unlock anything, a fragment of chalk, a glass stopper of a **decanter**, a tin soldier, a couple of tadpoles, six fire-crackers, a kitten with only one eye, a brass door-knob, a dog-collar—but no dog—the handle of a knife, four pieces of orange-peel, and a **dilapidated** old window sash.

30   He had had a nice, good, idle time all the while—plenty of company—and the fence had three coats of whitewash on it! If he hadn't run out of whitewash he would have bankrupted every boy in the village.

31   Tom said to himself that it was not such a hollow world, after all. He had discovered a great law of human action, without knowing it—namely, that in order to make a man or a boy covet a thing, it is only necessary to make the

NOTES

thing difficult to attain. If he had been a great and wise philosopher, like the writer of this book, he would now have comprehended that Work consists of whatever a body is OBLIGED to do, and that Play consists of whatever a body is not obliged to do. And this would help him to understand why constructing artificial flowers or performing on a tread-mill is work, while rolling ten-pins or climbing Mont Blanc is only amusement. There are wealthy gentlemen in England who drive four-horse passenger-coaches twenty or thirty miles on a daily line, in the summer, because the privilege costs them considerable money; but if they were offered wages for the service, that would turn it into work and then they would resign.

32　The boy mused awhile over the substantial change which had taken place in his worldly circumstances, and then **wended** toward headquarters to report.

THINK QUESTIONS　CA-CCSS: CA.RI.8.1, CA.L.8.4a, CA.SL.8.1c, CA.SL.8.1d

1. What kind of inspiration bursts upon Tom Sawyer as he returns his "straitened means" to his pocket at the beginning of the excerpt? Refer to evidence in the text to explain your answer.

2. After Ben first asks Tom to let him whitewash, why does Tom keep stalling, seeming about to consent and then suddenly changing his mind more than once? Refer to evidence in the text to explain your answer.

3. What does Tom learn about the difference between work and play at the end of the excerpt? Cite evidence from the text to support your answer.

4. Use context to determine the meaning of the word **dilapidated** as it is used in The Adventures of Tom Sawyer. Write your definition of "dilapidated" and tell how you found it.

5. Determine the meaning of the word **alacrity** as it is used in The Adventures of Tom Sawyer using context clues in the text. Write your definition of "alacrity" and tell how you found it.

CLOSE READ

CA-CCSS: CA.RL.8.1, CA.RL.8.3, CA.RL.8.6, CA.RL.8.7, CA.W.8.4, CA.W.8.5, CA.W.8.6, CA.W.8.10

Reread the excerpt from *The Adventures of Tom Sawyer*. As you reread, complete the Focus Questions below. Then use your answers and annotations from the questions to help you complete the Writing Prompt.

FOCUS QUESTIONS

1. How do the first two paragraphs of *The Adventures of Tom Sawyer* indicate that the narrator is using a third-person omniscient point of view? Highlight evidence from the text and make annotations to support your explanation.

2. After Ben starts whitewashing, Twain writes that Tom "planned the slaughter of more innocents," and then continues: "There was no lack of material; boys happened along every little while; they came to jeer, but remained to whitewash. By the time Ben was fagged out, Tom had traded the next chance to Billy Fisher for a kite, in good repair; and when he played out, Johnny Miller bought in for a dead rat and a string to swing it with—and so on, and so on, hour after hour. And when the middle of the afternoon came, from being a poor poverty-stricken boy in the morning, Tom was literally rolling in wealth." How does the film take these plot events and condense, or reduce them, into a single, brief shot lasting only a few seconds? Cite evidence from the film to support your answer.

3. At the end of the excerpt, how does using third-person omniscient point of view allow the author, Mark Twain, to reveal not only what Tom Sawyer has learned from his experience, but also a general rule about human behavior? Highlight textual evidence to support your ideas and write annotations to explain your choices.

4. Mark Twain utilizes the omniscient narrator in *The Adventures of Tom Sawyer* to create humor. How does he accomplish this? Cite textual evidence and evidence from the film to support your ideas.

5. How does Tom's life experience shape his values? Cite evidence from the text to support your answer.

WRITING PROMPT

Dramatic irony occurs when the words and actions of the characters in a work of literature have a different meaning for the reader than they do for the characters. This happens when readers have more knowledge about what its taking place than the characters themselves. How does Mark Twain use dramatic irony to create humor in *The Adventures of Tom Sawyer*? Use evidence from the story to support your response.

Please note that excerpts and passages in the StudySync® library and this workbook are intended as touchstones to generate interest in an author's work. The excerpts and passages do not substitute for the reading of entire texts, and StudySync strongly recommends that students seek out and purchase the whole literary or informational work in order to experience it as the author intended. Links to online resellers are available in our digital library. In addition, complete works may be ordered through an authorized reseller by filling out and returning to StudySync® the order form enclosed in this workbook.

Reading & Writing Companion 45

BORN WORKER

FICTION

Gary Soto

1998

INTRODUCTION

Mexican-American author Gary Soto grew up in California's Central Valley and worked as a field laborer before becoming a distinguished writer and professor. Soto draws inspiration from Latino poets to write about his experiences as farm worker and to describe the daily lives of his characters. In this short story, Soto explores the Mexican-American experience through two teenaged cousins and business partners, José and Arnie. Despite coming from the same family, differences in lifestyle and values emerge when José reluctantly agrees to work with his cousin and an emergency occurs at the work site.

"...his palms were already rough by the time he was three..."

 FIRST READ

1   They said that José was born with a ring of dirt around his neck, with grime under his fingernails, and skin calloused from the grainy twist of a shovel. They said his palms were already rough by the time he was three, and soon after he learned his primary color, his squint was the squint of an aged laborer. They said he was a born worker. By seven he was drinking coffee slowly, his mouth pursed the way his mother sipped. He wore jeans, a shirt with sleeves rolled to his elbows. His eye could measure a length of board, and his knees **genuflected** over flower beds and leafy gutters.

2   They said lots of things about José, but almost nothing of his parents. His mother stitched at a machine all day, and his father, with a steady job at the telephone company, climbed splintered, sun-sucked poles, fixed wires and looked around the city at tree level.

3   "What do you see up there?" José once asked his father.

4   "Work," he answered. "I see years of work, *mi'jo.*"

5   José took this as a truth, and though he did well in school, he felt destined to labor. His arms would pump, his legs would bend, his arms would carry a world of earth. He believed in hard work, believed that his strength was as ancient as a rock's.

6   "Life is hard," his father repeated from the time José could first make out the meaning of words until he was stroking his fingers against the grain of his sandpaper beard.

7   His mother was an example to José. She would raise her hands, showing her fingers pierced from the sewing machines. She bled on her machine, bled because there was money to make, a child to raise, and a roof to stay under.

Please note that excerpts and passages in the StudySync® library and this workbook are intended as touchstones to generate interest in an author's work. The excerpts and passages do not substitute for the reading of entire texts, and StudySync® strongly recommends that students seek out and purchase the whole literary or informational work in order to experience it as the author intended. Links to online resellers are available in our digital library. In addition, complete works may be ordered through an authorized reseller by filling out and returning to StudySync® the order form enclosed in this workbook.

Reading & Writing Companion   **47**

8   One day when José returned home from junior high, his cousin Arnie was sitting on the lawn sucking on a stalk of grass. José knew that grass didn't come from his lawn. His was cut and pampered, clean.

9   "José!" Arnie shouted as he took off the earphones of his CD Walkman.

10 "Hi, Arnie," José said without much enthusiasm. He didn't like his cousin. He thought he was lazy and, worse, spoiled by the trappings of being middle class. His parent had good jobs in offices and showered him with clothes, shoes, CDs, vacations, almost anything he wanted. Arnie's family had never climbed a telephone pole to size up the future.

11 Arnie rose to his feet, and José saw that his cousin was wearing a new pair of high-tops. He didn't say anything.

12 "Got an idea," Arnie said cheerfully. "Something that'll make us money."

13 José looked at his cousin, not a muscle of curiosity twitching in his face.

14 Still, Arnie explained that since he himself was so clever with words, and his best cousin in the whole world was good at working with his hands, that maybe they might start a company.

15 "What would you do?" José asked.

16 "Me?" he said brightly. "Shoot, I'll round up all kinds of jobs for you. You won't have to do anything." He stopped, then started again. "Except—you know—do the work."

17 "Get out of here," José said.

18 "Don't be that way," Arnie begged. "Let me tell you how it works."

19 The boys went inside the house, and while José stripped off his school clothes and put on his jeans and a T-shirt, Arnie told him that they could be rich.

20 "You ever hear of this guy named Bechtel?" Arnie asked.

21 José shook his head.

22 "Man, he started just like us," Arnie said. "He started digging ditches and stuff, and the next thing you knew, he was sitting by his own swimming pool. You want to sit by your own pool, don't you?" Arnie smiled, waiting for José to speak up.

NOTES

23   "Never heard of this guy Bechtel," José said after he rolled on two huge socks, worn at the heels. He opened up his chest of drawers and brought out a packet of Kleenex.

24   Arnie looked at the Kleenex.

25   "How come you don't use your sleeve?" Arnie joked.

26   José thought for a moment and said, "I'm not like you." He smiled at his retort.

27   "Listen, I'll find the work, and then we can split it fifty-fifty."

28   José knew fifty-fifty was a bad deal.

29   "How about sixty-forty?" Arnie suggested when he could see that José wasn't going for it. "I know a lot of people from my dad's job. They're waiting for us."

30   José sat on the edge of his bed and started to lace up his boots. He knew that there were agencies that would find you work, agencies that took a portion of your pay. They're cheats, he thought, people who sit in air-conditioned offices while others work.

31   "You really know a lot of people?" José asked.

32   "Boatloads," Arnie said. "My dad works with this millionaire—honest—who cooks a steak for his dog every day."

33   He's a liar, José thought. No matter how he tried, he couldn't picture a dog grubbing on steak. The world was too poor for that kind of silliness.

34   "Listen, I'll go eighty-twenty." José said.

35   "Aw, man," Arnie whined. "That ain't fair."

36   José laughed.

37   "I mean, half the work is finding the jobs," Arnie explained, his palms up as he begged José to be reasonable.

38   José knew this was true. He had had to go door-to-door, and he disliked asking for work. He assumed that it should automatically be his since he was a good worker, honest, and always on time.

39   "Where did you get this idea, anyhow?" José asked.

40   "I got a business mind," Arnie said proudly.

NOTES

41   "Just like that Bechtel guy," José retorted.

42   "That's right."

43   José agreed to a seventy-thirty split, with the condition that Arnie had to help out. Arnie hollered, arguing that some people were meant to work and others to come up with brilliant ideas. He was one of the latter. Still, he agreed after José said it was that or nothing.

44   In the next two weeks, Arnie found an array of jobs. José peeled off shingles from a rickety garage roof, carried rocks down a path to where a pond would go, and spray-painted lawn furniture. And while Arnie accompanied him, most of the time he did nothing. He did help occasionally. He did shake the cans of spray paint and kick aside debris so that José didn't trip while going down the path carrying the rocks. He did stack the piles of shingles, but almost cried when a nail bit his thumb. But mostly he told José what he had missed or where the work could be improved. José was bothered because he and his work had never been criticized before.

45   But soon José learned to ignore his cousin, ignore his comments about his spray painting, or about the way he lugged rocks, two in each arm. He didn't say anything, either, when they got paid and Arnie rubbed his hands like a fly, muttering, "It's payday."

46   Then Arnie found a job scrubbing a drained swimming pool. The two boys met early at José's house. Arnie brought his bike. José's own bike had a flat that grinned like a clown's face.

47   "I'll pedal," José suggested when Arnie said that he didn't have much leg strength.

48   With Arnie on the handlebars, José tore off, his pedaling so strong that tears of fear formed in Arnie's eyes.

49   "Slow down!" Arnie cried.

50   José ignored him and within minutes they were riding the bike up a gravel driveway. Arnie hopped off at first chance.

51   "You're scary," Arnie said, picking a gnat from his eye.

52   José chuckled.

53   When Arnie knocked on the door, an old man still in pajamas appeared in the window. He motioned for the boys to come around to the back.

NOTES

54 "Let me do the talking," Arnie suggested to his cousin. "He knows my dad real good. They're like this." He pressed two fingers together.

55 José didn't bother to say OK. He walked the bike into the backyard, which was lush with plants—roses in their last bloom, geraniums, hydrangeas, pansies with their skirts of bright colors. José could make out the splash of a fountain. Then he heard the hysterical yapping of a poodle. From all his noise, a person might have thought the dog was on fire.

56 "Hi, Mr. Clemens," Arnie said, extending his hand. "I'm Arnie Sanchez. It's nice to see you again."

57 José had never seen a kid actually greet someone like this. Mr. Clemens said, hiking up his pajama bottoms, "I only wanted one kid to work."

58 "Oh," Arnie stuttered. "Actually, my cousin José really does the work and I kind of, you know, supervise."

59 Mr. Clemens pinched up his wrinkled face. He seemed not to understand. He took out a pea-sized hearing aid, fiddled with its tiny dial, and fit it into his ear, which was surrounded with wiry gray hair.

60 "I'm only paying for one boy," Mr. Clemens shouted. His poodle click-clicked and stood behind his legs. The dog bared its small crooked teeth.

61 "That's right," Arnie said, smiling a strained smile. "we know that you're going to **compensate** only one of us."

62 Mr. Clemens muttered under his breath. He combed his hair with his fingers. He showed José the pool, which was shaped as round as an elephant. It was filthy with grime. Near the bottom some grayish water shimmered and leaves floated as limp as cornflakes.

63 "It's got to be real clean," Mr. Clemens said, "or it's not worth it."

64 "Oh, José's a great worker," Arnie said. He patted his cousin's shoulders and said that he could lift a mule.

65 Mr. Clemens sized up José and squeezed his shoulders, too.

66 "How do I know you, anyhow?" Mr. Clemens asked Arnie, who was aiming a smile at the poodle.

67 "You know my dad," Arnie answered, raising his smile to the old man. "He works at Interstate Insurance. You and he had some business deals."

Please note that excerpts and passages in the StudySync® library and this workbook are intended as touchstones to generate interest in an author's work. The excerpts and passages do not substitute for the reading of entire texts, and StudySync® strongly recommends that students seek out and purchase the whole literary or informational work in order to experience it as the author intended. Links to online resellers are available in our digital library. In addition, complete works may be ordered through an authorized reseller by filling out and returning to StudySync® the order form enclosed in this workbook.

Reading & Writing
Companion

51

68   Mr. Clemens thought for a moment, a hand on his mouth, head shaking. He could have been thinking about the meaning of life, his face was so dark.

69   "Mexican fella?" he inquired.

70   "That's him," Arnie said happily.

71   José felt like hitting his cousin for his cheerful attitude. Instead, he walked over and picked up the white plastic bottle of bleach. Next to it was a wire brush, a **pumice** stone, and some rags. He set down the bottle and, like a surgeon, put on a pair of rubber gloves.

72   "You know what you're doing, boy?" Mr. Clemens asked.

73   José nodded as he walked into the pool. If it had been filled with water, his chest would have been wet. The new hair on his chest would have been floating like the legs of a jellyfish.

74   "Oh, yeah," Arnie chimed, speaking for his cousin. "José was born to work."

75   José would have drowned his cousin if there had been more water. Instead, he poured a bleach solution into a rag and swirled it over an area. He took the wire brush and scrubbed. The black algae came up like a foamy monster.

76   "We're a team," Arnie said to Mr. Clemens.

77   Arnie descended into the pool and took the bleach bottle from José. He held it for José and smiled up at Mr. Clemens, who, hands on hips, watched for a while, the poodle at his side. He cupped his ear, as if to pick up the sounds of José's scrubbing.

78   "Nice day, huh?" Arnie sang.

79   "What?" Mr. Clemens said.

80   "Nice day," Arnie repeated, this time louder. "So which ear can't you hear in?" Grinning, Arnie wiggled his ear to make sure that Mr. Clemens knew what he was asking.

81   Mr. Clemens ignored Arnie. He watched José, whose arms worked back and forth like he was sawing logs.

82   "We're not only a team," Arnie shouted, "but we're also cousins."

83   Mr. Clemens shook his head at Arnie. When he left, the poodle leading the way, Arnie immediately climbed out of the pool and sat on the edge, legs dangling.

84 "It's going to be blazing," Arnie complained. He shaded his eyes with his hand and looked east, where the sun was rising over a sycamore, its leaves hanging like bats.

85 José scrubbed. He worked the wire brush over the black and green stains, the grime dripping like tears. He finished a large area. He hopped out of the pool and returned hauling a garden hose with an attached nozzle. He gave the cleaned area a blast. When the spray got too close, his cousin screamed, got up, and, searching for something to do, picked a **loquat** from a tree.

86 "What's your favorite fruit?" Arnie asked.

87 José ignored him.

88 Arnie stuffed a bunch of loquats into his mouth, then cursed himself for splattering juice on his new high-tops. He returned to the pool, his cheeks fat with the seeds, and once again sat at the edge. He started to tell José how he had first learned to swim. "We were on vacation in Mazatlán. You been there, ain't you?

89 José shook his head. He dabbed the bleach solution onto the sides of the pool with a rag and scrubbed a new area.

90 "Anyhow, my dad was on the beach and saw this drowned dead guy," Arnie continued. "And right there, my dad got scared and realized I couldn't swim."

91 Arnie rattled on about how his father had taught him in the hotel pool and later showed him where the drowned man's body had been.

92 "Be quiet," José said.

93 "What?"

94 "I can't concentrate," José said, stepping back to look at the cleaned area.

95 Arnie shut his mouth but opened it to lick loquat juice from his fingers. He kicked his legs against the swimming pool, bored. He looked around the backyard and spotted a lounge chair. He got up, dusting off the back of his pants, and threw himself into the cushions. He raised and lowered the back of the lounge. Sighing, he snuggled in. He stayed quiet for three minutes, during which time José scrubbed. His arms hurt but he kept working with long strokes. José knew that in an hour the sun would drench the pool with light. He hurried to get the job done.

96 Arnie then asked, "You ever peel before?"

97 José looked at his cousin. His nose burned from the bleach. He scrunched up his face.

98 "You know, like when you get sunburned."

99 "I'm too dark to peel," José said, his words echoing because he had advanced to the deep end. "Why don't you be quiet and let me work?"

100 Arnie babbled on that he had peeled when on vacation in Hawaii. He explained that he was really more French than Mexican, and that's why his skin was sensitive. He said that when he lived in France, people thought that he could be Portuguese or maybe Armenian, never Mexican.

101 José felt like soaking his rag with bleach and pressing it over Arnie's mouth to make him be quiet.

102 Then Mr. Clemens appeared. He was dressed in white pants and flowery shirt. His thin hair was combed so that his scalp, as pink as a crab, showed.

103 "I'm just taking a little rest," Arnie said.

104 Arnie leaped back into the pool. He took the bleach bottle and held it. He smiled at Mr. Clemens, who came to inspect their progress.

105 "José's doing a good job," Arnie said, then whistled a song.

106 Mr. Clemens peered into the pool, hands on knees, admiring the progress.

107 "Pretty good, huh?" Arnie asked.

108 Mr. Clemens nodded. Then his hearing aid fell out, and José turned in time to see it roll like a bottle cap toward the bottom of the pool. It leaped into the stagnant water with a plop. A single bubble went up, and it was gone.

109 "Dang," Mr. Clemens swore. He took shuffling steps toward the deep end. He steadied his gaze on where the hearing aid had sunk. He leaned over and suddenly, arms waving, one leg kicking out, he tumbled into the pool. He landed standing up, then his legs buckled, and he crumbled, his head striking against the bottom. He rolled once, and half of his body settled in the water.

110 "Did you see that!" Arnie shouted, big-eyed.

111 José had already dropped his brushes on the side of the pool and hurried to the old man, who moaned, eyes closed, his false teeth jutting from his mouth. A ribbon of blood immediately began to flow from his scalp.

112 "We better get out of here!" Arnie suggested. "They're going to blame us!"

NOTES

113 José knelt on both knees at the old man's side. He took the man's teeth from his mouth and placed them in his shirt pocket. The old man groaned and opened his eyes, which were shiny wet. He appeared startled, like a newborn.

114 "Sir, you'll be all right," José cooed, then snapped at his cousin. "Arnie, get over here and help me!"

115 "I'm going home," Arnie whined.

116 "You punk!" José yelled. "Go inside and call 911."

117 Arnie said that they should leave him there.

118 "Why should we get involved?" he cried as he started for his bike. "It's his own fault."

119 José laid the man's head down and with giant steps leaped out of the pool, shoving his cousin as he passed. He went into the kitchen and punched in 911 on a telephone. He explained to the operator what had happened. When asked the address, José dropped the phone and went onto the front porch to look for it.

120 "It's 940 East Brown," José breathed. He hung up and looked wildly about the kitchen. He opened up the refrigerator and brought out a plastic tray of ice, which he twisted so that a few of the cubes popped out and slid across the floor. He wrapped some cubes in a dish towel. When he raced outside, Arnie was gone, the yapping poodle was doing laps around the edge of the pool, and Mr. Clemens was trying to stand up.

121 "No, sir," José said as he jumped into the pool, his own knees almost buckling. "Please, sit down."

122 Mr. Clemens staggered and collapsed. José caught him before he hit his head again. The towel of ice cubes dropped from his hands. With his legs spread to absorb the weight, José raised the man up in his arms, this fragile man. He picked him up and carefully stepped toward the shallow end, one slow elephant step at a time.

123 "You'll be all right," José said, more to himself than to Mr. Clemens, who moaned and struggled to be let free.

124 The sirens wailed in the distance. The poodle yapped, which started a dog barking in the neighbor's yard.

125 "You'll be OK," José repeated, and in the shallow end of the pool, he edged up the steps. He lay the old man in the lounge chair and raced back inside for more ice and another towel. He returned outside and placed the bundle of cubes on the man's head, where the blood flowed. Mr. Clemens was awake,

NOTES

looking about. When the old man felt his mouth, José reached into his shirt pocket and pulled out his false teeth. He fit the teeth into Mr. Clemens's mouth and a smile appeared, something bright at a difficult time.

126 "I hit my head," Mr. Clemens said after smacking his teeth so that the fit was right.

127 José looked up and his gaze floated to a telephone pole, one his father might have climbed. If he had been there, his father would have seen that José was more than just a good worker. He would have seen a good man. He held the towel to the old man's head. The poodle, now quiet, joined them on the lounge chair.

128 A fire truck pulled into the driveway and soon they were surrounded by firemen, one of whom brought out a first-aid kit. A fireman led José away and asked what happened. He was starting to explain when his cousin reappeared, yapping like a poodle.

129 "I was scrubbing the pool," Arnie shouted, "and I said, 'Mr. Clemens, you shouldn't stand so close to the edge.' But did he listen? No, he leaned over and . . . Well, you can just imagine my horror."

130 José walked away from Arnie's **jabbering**. He walked away, and realized that there were people like his cousin, the liar, and people like himself, someone he was getting to know. He walked away and in the midmorning heat boosted himself up a telephone pole. He climbed up and saw for himself what his father saw—miles and miles of trees and houses, and a future lost in the layers of yellowish haze.

THINK QUESTIONS   CA-CCSS: CA.RL.8.1, CA.RL.8.4, CA.L.8.4a, CA.L.8.4c, CA.L.8.4d

1. Why do you think José feels he is "destined to labor"? Support your answer with textual evidence.

2. José doesn't like his cousin Arnie, so why does he decide to go into business with him? Support your answer with textual evidence.

3. Use details from the text to cite some of the major differences between Arnie and José.

4. Use context to determine the meaning of the word **genuflected** as it is used in "Born Worker." Write your definition of "genuflected" and explain how you found it.

5. Use context to determine the meaning of the word **jabbering** as it is used in "Born Worker." Write your definition of "jabbering" and show how you found it. Check your answer against the dictionary definition.

CLOSE READ
CA-CCSS: CA.RL.8.1, CA.RL.8.2, CA.RL.8.3, CA.RL.8.4, CA.RL.8.5, CA.RL.8.9, CA.W.8.4, CA.W.8.5, CA.W.8.6, CA.W.8.10

Reread the short story "Born Worker." As you reread, complete the Focus Questions below. Then use your answers and annotations from the questions to help you complete the Writing Prompt.

FOCUS QUESTIONS

1. As trickster archetypes, how do Arnie (in this story) and Tom Sawyer (in *The Adventures of Tom Sawyer)* both use lies and deception to get what they want? Use textual evidence from both texts to support your answer.

2. José doesn't like his cousin because he feels Arnie is "lazy and, worse, spoiled by the trappings of being middle class." What details does the author include in the story that reveal how Arnie really feels about José? Does he see José as his equal? Support your answer with textual evidence.

3. Highlight the paragraph that presents the climax of the story. What do the characters' responses to this event reveal about both José and Arnie, and how are their responses linked to the theme of the story? Cite textual evidence to support your answer.

4. José's father works for the telephone company, and throughout the story, Gary Soto refers to telephone poles. What is the significance of the telephone pole as the author uses it in the story? How does it relate to the theme? Cite textual evidence to support your answer.

5. How does José's experience with Mr. Clemens shape, and ultimately change, his values? How does it compare to what Tom Sawyer realizes after his whitewashing experience? Highlight evidence from both texts and make annotations to support your answer.

WRITING PROMPT

Read the excerpt from *The Adventures of Tom Sawyer.* Think about how both Tom Sawyer and Arnie Sanchez represent the trickster, a deceptive character who acts in a way that opposes conventional behavior. Write a short essay in which you compare and contrast Tom and Arnie. Who is more likeable, Tom or Arnie? Cite evidence from both texts to support your response.

ODE TO THANKS

POETRY
Pablo Neruda
1995

INTRODUCTION

Chilean-born Pablo Neruda is an internationally recognized poet who was awarded the Nobel Prize in Literature in 1971. His poetry provides descriptions of everyday objects and events as well as reflections about grand ideas. In his poem "Ode to Thanks," Neruda pays tribute to the word *thanks*.

"Your light brightens the altar of harshness."

FIRST READ

1 Thanks to the word
2 that says *thanks!*
3 Thanks to *thanks,*
4 word
5 that melts
6 iron and snow!

7 The world is a threatening place
8 until
9 *thanks*
10 makes the rounds
11 from one pair of lips to another,
12 soft as a bright
13 feather
14 and sweet as a petal of sugar,
15 filling the mouth with its sound
16 or else a **mumbled**
17 whisper.
18 Life becomes human again:
19 it's no longer an open window.
20 A bit of brightness
21 strikes into the forest,
22 and we can sing again beneath the leaves.
23 *Thanks,* you're the medicine we take
24 to save us from
25 the bite of **scorn.**
26 Your light brightens the **altar** of harshness.

27 Or maybe
28 a **tapestry**

29 known
30 to far distant peoples.
31 Travelers
32 fan out
33 into the wilds,
34 and in the jungle
35 of strangers,
36 *merci*
37 rings out
38 while the hustling train
39 changes countries,
40 sweeping away borders,
41 then *spasibo*
42 **clinging** to pointy
43 volcanoes, to fire and freezing cold,
44 or *danke,* yes! and *gracias,* and
45 the world turns into a table:
46 a single word has wiped it clean,
47 plates and glasses gleam,
48 silverware tinkles,
49 and the tablecloth is as broad as a plain.

50 Thank you, *thanks,*
51 for going out and returning,
52 for rising up
53 and settling down.
54 We know, *thanks,*
55 that you don't fill every space-
56 you're only a word-
57 but
58 where your little petal
59 appears
60 the daggers of pride take cover,
61 and there's a penny's worth of smiles.

From *Ode to Opposites* by Pablo Neruda, translated by Ken Krabbenhoft . Odes (Spanish) copyright © 1995 by Pablo Neruda and Fundación Pablo Neruda; Odes (English translation) copyright © 1995 by Ken Krabbenhoft; Illustrations and compilation copyright © 1995 by Ferris Cook. Used by permission of Bullfinch/Hachette Book Group USA.

Pablo Neruda, "Oda a las gracias", NAVEGACIONES Y REGRESOS @ Fundación Pablo Neruda

 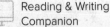

THINK QUESTIONS   CA-CCSS: CA.RL.8.1, CA.L.8.4a, CA.L.8.4c

1. How does the word *thanks* make the speaker of the poem feel, and why? Cite textual evidence to support your answer.

2. Why does the poet use the word *thanks* in different languages? Cite textual evidence to support your reason.

3. At the end of the poem, to what does the poet compare the word *thanks,* and why? Use textual evidence to support your answer.

4. Use context to determine the meaning of the word **scorn** as it is used in "Ode to Thanks." Write your definition of "scorn" and tell how you got it.

5. The speaker says that *thanks* is "a tapestry known to far distant peoples." What does the context tell you about the meaning of the word **tapestry?** Use textual evidence to explain. Then look up "tapestry" in a dictionary and compare what you learned about the word with the one in the dictionary. How does the dictionary definition help you understand the meaning of the line?

CLOSE READ

CA-CCSS: CA.RL.8.1, CA.RL.8.2, CA.RL.8.4, CA.RL.8.5

Reread the poem "Ode to Thanks." As you reread, complete the Focus Questions below. Then use your answers and annotations from the questions to help you complete the Writing Prompt.

FOCUS QUESTIONS

1. In the second stanza, or section, of "Ode to Thanks," what does the speaker mean when he says, "Life becomes human again"? How is this a result of expressing thanks? How does the structure of this stanza develop this idea? Highlight evidence from the poem to support your response and make annotations to explain your choices.

2. In the third stanza of "Ode to Thanks," what is the impact of describing *thanks* in so many different languages? How do images such as the "hustling train" and "clinging to pointy volcanoes, to fire and freezing cold" add to the impact? Highlight textual evidence to support your answer. Make annotations to explain how these images and their part in the poetic structure of the stanza help Neruda further his idea of praising *thanks*.

3. In the fourth stanza of "Ode to Thanks," what does the speaker mean when he says "Thank you, *thanks*, / for going out and returning, / for rising up / and settling down"? What images come to mind, and how does the structuring of

the images affect the meaning of the poem? Highlight textual evidence to support your answer. Make annotations to explain your ideas.

4. Think about the poet's message or theme in "Ode to Thanks." How might the simple act of saying the word *thanks* help to shape people's values? How does each stanza of the poem help to develop this theme? Highlight textual evidence and make annotations to explain your ideas.

5. Just as Pablo Neruda, in his poem "Ode to Thanks" gives thanks to the concept of giving thanks, author Rudolfo Anaya celebrates something important by giving thanks, too, in his essay "A Celebration of Grandfathers." Why do you think Neruda uses the form of a poem to celebrate his subject, while Anaya uses the form of an essay? Compare and contrast the structures of the two texts to explain how the differing structures contribute to each author's meaning and style. Highlight textual evidence and make annotations to explain your ideas.

WRITING PROMPT

In "Ode to Thanks," how does poet Pablo Neruda invite readers to appreciate the concept of gratitude? In an essay of at least 300 words, explain how the poetic structure, as well as the poet's use of connotative word meanings and figurative language, help you understand the poem's message. If you were to write your own ode in the style of Pablo Neruda, what would you praise, and why?

Reading & Writing Companion

THE LITTLE BOY LOST/ THE LITTLE BOY FOUND

POETRY
William Blake
1789

INTRODUCTION

illiam Blake was an 18th century British artist and poet known in part for his richly illustrated poetry collections *Songs of Innocence* and *Songs of Experience*. As the two titles suggest, Blake viewed the world in contrasts. The poems in *Songs of Innocence* focus on the naivety and simplicity of youth, while the poems from the later *Experience* volume explore the darker, corrupted side of human nature. "The Little Boy Lost" and "The Little Boy Found" are from *Songs of Innocence*.

"The night was dark, no father was there..."

 FIRST READ

"The Little Boy Lost"

1. "Father, father, where are you going?
2. O do not walk so fast!
3. Speak, father, speak to your little boy,
4. Or else I shall be lost."

5. The night was dark, no father was there;
6. The child was wet with dew;
7. The mire was deep, & the child did weep,
8. And away the vapour flew.

"The Little Boy Found"

9. The little boy lost in the lonely **fen**,
10. Led by the wand'ring light,
11. Began to cry, but God, ever **nigh,**
12. Appeared like his father, in white.

13. He kissed the child, & by the hand led
14. And to his mother brought,
15. Who in sorrow pale, thro' the lonely **dale;**
16. Her little boy weeping sought.

THINK QUESTIONS
CA-CCSS: CA.RL.8.1, CA.L.8.4a, CA.SL.8.1a, CA.SL.8.1b, CA.SL.8.1d

1. Summarize what the speaker in the first stanza, or section, is saying in the poem "The Little Boy Lost." What do you think is happening in the poem? Support your understanding both from ideas that are directly stated and ideas that you have inferred from clues in the text.

2. Summarize what the speaker is saying in the first stanza of "The Little Boy Found." Use details from the poem to write two or three sentences explaining what has happened to the little boy in the second stanza. Support your understanding both from ideas that are directly stated and ideas that you have inferred from clues in the text.

3. Who do you think the "father" is in these two poems? Write two or three sentences exploring the idea of the "father" in the two poems. Support your answer with textual evidence from both poems.

4. Use context to determine the meaning of the word **mire** as it is used in "The Little Boy Lost." Write your definition of "mire" and explain how you figured it out. Also explain its effect in the poem.

5. Use context to determine the meaning of the word **nigh** as it is used in "The Little Boy Found." Write your definition of nigh and state the clue(s) from the text you used to determine your answer.

CLOSE READ

CA-CCSS: CA.RL.8.1, CA.RL.8.2, CA.RL.8.4, CA.L.8.5c, CA.W.8.4, CA.W.8.5, CA.W.8.6, CA.W.8.10

Reread the poems "The Little Boy Lost/The Little Boy Found." As you reread, complete the Focus Questions below. Then use your answers and annotations from the questions to help you complete the Writing Prompt.

FOCUS QUESTIONS

1. The first stanza of "The Little Boy Lost" is not really descriptive, but it still creates a vivid image in the reader's mind. Explain how you visualized what is happening in the stanza and what parts of the text helped create your visualization. Support your answer with textual evidence and make annotations to explain your choices.

2. Explain how the poet creates a tone of unease and eeriness in "The Little Boy Lost," through the use of figurative language, connotative word meanings, and other word choices. Highlight evidence from the text and make annotations to explain your answer.

3. What is the tone of the first lines of "The Little Boy Found"? What figurative language, connotative word meanings, and word choices help to create the tone? Highlight evidence from the text and make annotations to explain your answer.

4. How does the tone change over the two stanzas of "The Little Boy Found"? What words and phrases help create the new tone? Highlight your textual evidence and make annotations to explain your answer.

5. What important life experiences does the boy have as Blake depicts them in "The Little Boy Lost" and "The Little Boy Found"? How might these experiences affect the boy and shape his values? Make annotations stating your inferences about the poems and their deeper meanings. Highlight textual evidence and make annotations to explain your ideas.

WRITING PROMPT

The poems "The Little Boy Lost" and "The Little Boy Found" by William Blake are, on the surface, about a child's responses to being left behind by his father and returned to his mother, with God's help. Think about what the poet might be saying about earthly life and spiritual life through these events. How do the words "lost" and "found" help develop the poems' themes? Use your understanding of figurative language and connotative meanings, as well as other textual evidence, to support your analysis.

A POISON TREE

POETRY

William Blake

1794

INTRODUCTION

William Blake was an 18th century British artist and poet known in part for his richly illustrated poetry collections *Songs of Innocence* and *Songs of Experience*. As the two titles suggest, Blake viewed the world in contrasts. The poems in *Songs of Innocence* focus on the naivety and simplicity of youth, while the poems from the later *Experience* volume explore the darker, corrupted side of human nature. "A Poison Tree" is from *Songs of Experience*.

"I water'd it in fears, Night & morning with my tears..."

 FIRST READ

1   I was angry with my friend:
2   I told my **wrath,** my wrath did end.
3   I was angry with my foe:
4   I told it not, my wrath did grow.

5   And I water'd it in fears,
6   Night & morning with my tears;
7   And I sunned it with smiles,
8   And with soft **deceitful wiles.**

9   And it grew both day and night,
10 Till it bore an apple bright;
11 And my foe **beheld** it shine,
12 And he knew that it was mine,

13 And into my garden stole
14 When the night had **veil'd** the pole;
15 In the morning glad I see
16 My foe outstretch'd beneath the tree.

THINK QUESTIONS   CA-CCSS: CA.RL.8.1, CA.RL.8.4, CA.L.8.4a

1. What emotion does the speaker discuss over the course of the poem? What accounts for the differences in the way he expresses it or deals with it? Support your answer with textual evidence.

2. How does the speaker of the poem behave toward others when he is angry with them? Support your inference with textual evidence.

3. What does the poem reveal about the foe? What does the poem **not** reveal about the foe? Support your answer with textual evidence.

4. Use context to determine the meaning of the word **wrath** as it is used in "A Poison Tree." Write your definition of "wrath" and tell how you found it.

5. Use the context clues provided in the passage to determine the meaning of **beheld.** You may also use your knowledge of word forms. Write your definition of "beheld" and tell how you got it.

CLOSE READ

CA-CCSS: CA.RL.8.1, CA.RL.8.2, CA.RL.8.4, CA.RL.8.9, CA.L.8.5b, CA.W.8.4, CA.W.8.5, CA.W.8.6, CA.W.8.9a, CA.W.8.10

Reread the poem "A Poison Tree." As you reread, complete the Focus Questions below. Then use your answers and annotations from the questions to help you complete the Writing Prompt.

FOCUS QUESTIONS

1. What is the relationship between the words "night" and "morning" in the second stanza, and "day and night" and the third stanza? Explain what these word pairs suggest about the speaker and how they add to the poem's meaning. Highlight textual evidence and annotate to explain your answer.

2. Write two or three sentences describing how allusion adds to the meaning of the third and fourth stanzas of "A Poison Tree." How is this allusion tied to the theme or message of the poem? Highlight textual evidence and write annotations to explain your answer.

3. In the last line of the poem, the foe is found "outstretch'd beneath the tree." What connotations does Blake's choice of the word "outstretch'd" (or outstretched), instead of a related word such as "lying" or "dead" or "motionless," add to the poem? Highlight relevant textual details and annotate to explain your ideas.

4. Think about the poem's title. How are the tree and the speaker's "wrath" related? State how the two things can be compared, including the type of figurative language the poet is using. Explain how this comparison contributes to the poem's meaning. Highlight textual evidence and write annotations to explain your analysis.

5. Based on the poem, what does the speaker value most and what guides his choices? What can you infer about the quality of the speaker's life based on his values? Finally, how do the poet's use of biblical allusions contribute to your understanding of the speaker? Highlight details in the poem and annotate to explain your inferences.

WRITING PROMPT

William Blake wrote "The Poison Tree" as part of a collection called *Songs of Experience*. What theme is most strongly present in "A Poison Tree"? Why is this poem a "song of experience"? Use textual evidence to explain your reasons and to support your claim. Include the poem's word relationships and figurative language, as well as your understanding of allusion, in your evidence.

MANDATORY VOLUNTEER WORK FOR TEENAGERS

NON-FICTION
2014

INTRODUCTION

I n these two articles, the writer make cases for and against making volunteer work a mandatory part of school curriculum. While volunteering can be a valuable experience that enriches the lives of both the volunteers and the people they help, some are concerned that forcing teens to volunteer may do more harm than good. Each article presents strong arguments and supports its claims with evidence. Which argument do you feel is more convincing?

"Everyone knows that volunteers make the United States a better place."

 FIRST READ

1 **Volunteer Work: Should We Make It a Requirement for Teens?**

2 **Point: Give Teens Some Work to Do! It's Good for Them and Everyone Else**

3 Teenagers today live in a confusing world. The media sends many mixed messages about what it means to be a helpful person in society. One of the best ways to help teens find their way is to make volunteer work a **mandatory** part of their school curriculum. Some people would immediately argue that this is an unnecessary action—many teens already volunteer without it being a requirement. It's true: teens have a **propensity** to volunteer more than adults. However, as a society we should make sure that not just some, but all, teens volunteer. Many of the teens that volunteer do so as part of a religious group or a youth leadership organization. In fact, 46 percent of teens who volunteer are working with a religious group or a youth leadership organization while only 18 percent of teens who volunteer are working with school-based groups. This shows that clearly the best way to include all teens in the benefits of volunteering is to add mandatory volunteer work to the school curriculum.

4 There are many benefits to volunteering. One obvious benefit is that volunteering helps the community—volunteers help the elderly, the disabled, and children. Furthermore, many people are able to receive food and medical assistance that they would not receive otherwise thanks to the hard work of volunteers. And let's not forget the environment! Volunteers make our world a cleaner place by doing things like picking up trash and teaching others about recycling. However, volunteering brings advantages that many people don't think of right away: benefits to the volunteers themselves! According to the United Way, volunteering helps people make important networking contacts, develop new skills, gain work experience, and enhance their resume. All of these benefits are crucial to teens who will soon be entering the workforce. The United Way also says that volunteering gives people the

opportunity to teach their skills to others and build self-esteem and confidence. These two benefits are helpful to teens who are developing their social skills. Finally, the United Way says that volunteering improves people's health and helps to make a difference in someone's life, benefits that are wonderful for volunteers at any age! The numerous advantages that come from volunteering definitely warrant making volunteering a compulsory part of school curriculum.

5   One very specific reason to tie volunteer work to education is that teen volunteers are more likely to succeed academically than teens who don't volunteer. Back in 2005, a collaborative study conducted by the Corporation for National and Community Service and the U.S. Census Bureau revealed that students who do better in school are more likely to be volunteers. There are numerous possible reasons for this trend. It may be because teenagers who volunteer learn new skills, or because the work helps teenagers build confidence, or because volunteering provides a sense of purpose. Whatever the reason, the abundantly clear link between students who volunteer and academic success is too important to be ignored.

6   What happens to teenagers who volunteer as they grow into adults? They continue to volunteer, of course! According to the United Way, volunteering as a youth will increase the chances that a person will volunteer as an adult, which makes sense given the many benefits of volunteering. Unfortunately, however, adults who were never encouraged to volunteer as youths may never start because they are oblivious of the benefits. A simple solution to this would be to make volunteer work a mandatory part of the school curriculum so that everyone will be provided the opportunity to be exposed to the helpful benefits of volunteering. Aside from the benefits to the individual volunteer, think about the benefit to society as a whole. Community service programs across the country will have a fresh new crop of enthusiastic, lifelong volunteers to count on. Everyone knows that volunteers make the United States a better place. The more volunteers, young and old, the better!

7   The evidence is clear: Volunteering is beneficial to both the community and the volunteers themselves. Because the advantages of volunteering so heavily outweigh the disadvantages, it makes sense to start people on a path of volunteerism early by making volunteering a mandatory part of the school curriculum.

8   **Counterpoint: Mandatory Volunteer Work Does More Harm Than Good**

9   Most people agree that teenagers today live in a difficult world. There are more pressures facing the modern teen than we can count: school, work, family, sports, and other extracurricular activities, just to name a few. However, some people think that we should add to that load of pressures by making volunteer work a mandatory part of the school curriculum. One of the greatest

arguments for this action is that mandatory volunteer work will prepare students for the future by giving them work experience, but the flaw in this logic is that many teens already gain work experience through paying jobs. In fact, many of the teens working paying jobs are doing so out of necessity— to pay for gas to get back and forth to school, or to help their families with extra money. Those teens without paying jobs still have plenty of prospects for gaining work experience in other ways such as an internship, or working at a school paper. Another argument for making volunteer work a mandatory part of school curriculum is that this work will help teens gain self-esteem and self-confidence. However, having time to socialize and develop hobbies and other interests is more important for self-esteem and self-confidence than volunteering.

10   The most compelling argument *against* making volunteer work a mandatory part of school curriculum is time. Teens today are just too busy to add another stressor to their lives. Let's take a look at twenty-four hours in the life of a typical teen. Allocate eight hours per day for sleep, eight hours for school (including getting ready and travel time), three hours for homework, two hours for activities such as sports or a part-time job, two hours for dinner and family time, and one hour for socializing. These activities take up all twenty-four hours leaving scarcely any time for volunteer work. Should students have to sacrifice their one hour of socializing per day, or sacrifice an hour of precious family time? These options just don't make sense as making more demands on teens' packed schedules can have serious side effects. Teens who are too busy feel tired, anxious, or depressed. Studies show they often have headaches or stomachaches due to stress, missed meals, or lack of sleep and they may fall behind in school, causing their grades to suffer. These drawbacks clearly outweigh the benefits of volunteering.

11   Another problem with making volunteer work a mandatory part of curriculum is that it defeats the purpose of volunteering in the first place. People volunteer because they have extra time and energy to give, and they genuinely want to help. Students that are forced to volunteer may resent the demand on their time, and therefore perform the work grudgingly. This will not help to make students feel useful or helpful, which would be counterproductive. Furthermore, students will not be able to experience the positive social benefits of volunteering because they see it as a requirement rather than a positive experience. Because of forced volunteer work, students may hesitate to explore volunteering as an adult. This is a huge drawback because there are genuine benefits to volunteering when someone actually has the time and means to do so.

12   Finally, there is great evidence that the teens that do have the time to volunteer already do! This eliminates the need to make volunteer work mandatory. In 2005, a collaborative study on the volunteering habits of

NOTES

teenagers conducted by the Corporation for National and Community Service and the U.S. Census Bureau revealed that an estimated 15.5 million teens between the ages of 12 and 18 do volunteer work. This is about 55 percent of youth, a number all the more astounding when compared to the meager 29 percent of adults who do volunteer work. They also found that young people complete more than 1.3 billion hours of volunteer work each year. These findings demonstrate that a significant number of teenagers are already participating in service to their communities when they are able. Since volunteer work is clearly popular among teenagers, it is safe to assume that the minority of teenagers who do not volunteer are only choosing not to participate because they do not have the time.

13　Making volunteer work a mandatory part of school curriculum may seem like a good idea at first glance. Volunteering is good for the community and offers many benefits for the person volunteering as well. However, upon further examination it becomes clear that this is not a good plan. Adding another time stressor into the lives of teenagers just isn't worth it.

THINK QUESTIONS   CA-CCSS: CA.RI.8.1, CA.RI.8.4, CA.L.8.4a

1. How do the first paragraphs of both essays serve as summaries for the entire essays? Cite words and phrases that show how each of the first paragraphs outlines the entire essays.

2. One way to draw inferences about writers' points of view is to make a list of the points they emphasize in a text. What points does the writer emphasize in each of the essays? Highlight these places in the text. What inferences can you draw from this evidence?

3. What kinds of evidence do the authors offer as support for their points? Do you think their support is effective? Highlight places in the text where evidence is introduced, and explain why you think it is effective or not effective.

4. Use context to determine the meaning of the word **grudgingly** as it is used in the third paragraph of "Counterpoint: Mandatory Volunteer Work Does More Harm Than Good." Write your definition of "grudgingly" and tell how you found it.

5. Use context to determine the meaning of the word **allocate** as it is used in the second paragraph of "Counterpoint: Mandatory Volunteer Work Does More Harm Than Good." Write your definition of "allocate" and tell how you found it.

Please note that excerpts and passages in the StudySync® library and this workbook are intended as touchstones to generate interest in an author's work. The excerpts and passages do not substitute for the reading of entire texts, and StudySync® strongly recommends that students seek out and purchase the whole literary or informational work in order to experience it as the author intended. Links to online resellers are available in our digital library. In addition, complete works may be ordered through an authorized reseller by filling out and returning to StudySync® the order form enclosed in this workbook.

Reading & Writing
Companion

75

CLOSE READ CA-CCSS: CA.RI.8.1, CA.RI.8.4, CA.RI.8.6, CA.RI.8.8, CA.RI.8.9, CA.W.8.4, CA.W.8.5, CA.W.8.6, CA.W.8.10, CA.SL.8.3

Reread the essays arguing for and against mandatory volunteer work for teenagers. As you reread, complete the Focus Questions below. Then use your answers and annotations from the questions to help you complete the Writing Prompt.

FOCUS QUESTIONS

1. Explain how the authors' points of view are shown in both the Point and the Counterpoint essay. Where do they exhibit conflicting evidence or viewpoints? Support your answer with textual evidence and make annotations to explain your answer choices.

2. Select one paragraph from the body of both the Point and the Counterpoint essays and compare and contrast how each author uses evidence to support his or her reasons. Which essay do you think does a better job of using evidence to support their reasons? Support your answer with textual evidence and make annotations to explain your answer choices.

3. Contrast the connotations, or emotional qualities, of language used in both of the essays. Use this information to describe the tone of each essay.

Highlight your textual evidence and make annotations to explain your descriptions.

4. Do you think that both Point and Counterpoint supporters might agree on any issues or ideas brought up in these essays? Explain and highlight your textual evidence and make annotations to explain your thoughts.

5. How do our own life experiences and preferences help us to determine what is work and what is play? According to the Counterpoint essay, mandating volunteer work could result in adults who are too resentful to volunteer. Do you agree with this warning? Why or why not? Highlight evidence, including the way the argument is structured, to support your ideas. Write annotations to explain your opinion.

WRITING PROMPT

Mark Twain's narrator in *The Adventures of Tom Sawyer* shares many ideas on the idea of working and volunteering. In the two essays that make up *Mandatory Volunteer Work for Teenagers,* what is each writer's point of view on teen volunteerism? What can you infer about the writers' values from the reasons and evidence presented in the Point and the Counterpoint? Compare and contrast the way reasons and evidence are presented in the two essays. Which essay do you think makes the most convincing arguments? Use textual evidence to support your opinion.

MOM'S FIRST DAY

English Language Development

FICTION

INTRODUCTION

Sometimes life takes you by surprise and challenges you without warning. When this happens, you rely on your values to pull you through. In "Mom's First Day," Yvette is startled when her mother addresses her in a familiar way in front of her classmates. In a flash, this innocent, awkward encounter swells into a moment of truth.

"I look up. There she is, in her favorite church outfit, standing in front of the class."

 FIRST READ

1   "Be nice to Mom today," my dad tells me, setting my sack lunch on the counter. It's not even 7:30 am on Monday and already I'm wishing the week were over. How will I possibly survive a week with my mother as my substitute teacher? "Make her feel welcome," my dad continues. "Remember what school felt like on *your* first day?"

2   Just then my mother enters the kitchen. As she **flutters** between the coffee pot and the refrigerator, she looks as nervous as the hummingbird that **hovers** outside the window. To my horror, she is dressed in one of her church outfits: a green silk dress with beige pumps. I am about to tell her she is *way* too **dressy** for school, when I remember my father's words.

3   None of this would be happening if Pepe hadn't been born. For years, Mom had a job teaching science at a private school in town, but she quit toward the end of her pregnancy. She's pretty much been home with Pepe ever since. If I were her, I'd want to get out of the house, too. Don't get me wrong, Pepe is cute and everything, but he cries a lot, and it's a safe bet there's something wet on his body at all times.

4   Lucky for me, my best friend Katie and I have science class together. We get there early and sit in the back. As the class fills up around us, I **slump** low in my seat and doodle in my notebook, keeping my head down. As the minutes tick by, my worries increase. What if people laugh at her? What if they laugh at me because she's my mom? Suddenly, everybody gets quiet.

5   I look up. There she is, in her favorite church outfit, standing in front of the class. For a moment, I think she is going to single me out, but she just gives me a little, knowing smile and starts her lesson.

NOTES

6 To my surprise, Mom does a good job. She even makes the class laugh a few times. But still I keep my eyes on the clock, praying for the hands to move faster.

7 Finally the bell rings. Katie and I jump up. We are almost out the door when I hear her.

8 "Yvette," she says. She's holding my sack lunch. "You forgot your lunch."

9 "Thanks," I mumble. I take it from her without meeting her eyes.

10 "Love you," says Mom, just like she often does, only this time it's in front of my classmates. Everybody freezes. I feel my cheeks start to burn. I'm so **humiliated**, all I can do is turn and bury my face in Katie's shoulder. To my relief, the kids around me start to laugh, and so I laugh, too. But then, almost by accident, I see the sad expression on my mother's face. Her disappointment hits like a **tidal wave**. I don't know what to call this new feeling, but I know I'll be left thinking about it for a long time.

⚙ USING LANGUAGE CA-CCSS: ELD.PI.8.6.c.Ex, ELD.PI.8.12.b.Ex

Read each word. Complete each row by filling in the correct root or affix meaning in the second column and definition in the third column.

Root/Affix Meaning Options		Definition Options
priv- meaning "separate"	*qui-* meaning "rest"	separate from others; being alone
super- meaning "above, over"	*sci-* meaning "know"	resting one's lips; not talking
viv- meaning "live"	*-ence* meaning "the state of having"	to live through or overcome something
		knowledge about the natural world

Word	Root/Affix Meaning	Definition
survive		
private		
science		
quiet		

🖥 Reading & Writing Companion

MEANINGFUL INTERACTIONS CA-CCSS: ELD.PI.8.1.Ex

Work with your group to discuss your first impressions of the text. First, take turns saying what you think about Yvette, Mom, and their relationship. Then, build on your peers' responses by asking questions and explaining why you agree or disagree with their ideas. Use the speaking frames to support your discussion. Last, use the self-assessment rubric to evaluate your participation in the discussion.

- I think Yvette is . . . because . . .

- In my opinion, Mom is . . . because . . .

- I would describe Yvette's relationship with Mom as . . . because . . .

- I think their relationship changes / does not change because . . .

- I think you said . . . Why do you think that?

- I agree / disagree because . . .

SELF-ASSESSMENT RUBRIC CA-CCSS: ELD.PI.8.1.Ex

	4 I did this well.	3 I did this pretty well.	2 I did this a little bit.	1 I did not do this.
I took an active part with others in doing the assigned task.				
I contributed effectively to the group's discussion.				
I waited my turn to speak.				
I asked group members questions about their ideas.				
I built on my group members' responses by explaining why I agreed or disagreed with their ideas.				

Please note that excerpts and passages in the StudySync® library and this workbook are intended as touchstones to generate interest in an author's work. The excerpts and passages do not substitute for the reading of entire texts, and StudySync® strongly recommends that students seek out and purchase the whole literary or informational work in order to experience it as the author intended. Links to online resellers are available in our digital library. In addition, complete works may be ordered through an authorized reseller by filling out and returning to StudySync® the order form enclosed in this workbook.

Reading & Writing Companion

81

REREAD

Reread paragraphs 1–3 of "Mom's First Day." After you reread, complete the Using Language and Meaningful Interactions activities.

USING LANGUAGE   CA-CCSS: ELD.PII.8.1.Ex

Complete the chart by arranging the events from the story into chronological order, starting with what happens first and ending with what happens last.

Event Options	
Mom quits her job.	Mom stays home with Pepe.
Mom becomes a substitute teacher at Yvette's school.	Mom teaches at a private school.

First	Next	Then	Last

MEANINGFUL INTERACTIONS CA-CCSS: ELD.PI.8.1.Ex

Based on what you have read in "Mom's First Day," describe the conflict between Yvette and her mother. What happened? How do the characters feel about it? Whose fault is it? In small groups, identify and paraphrase details from the text about the events and feelings that led to the conflict. Use the writing frames to support your discussion. Then, use the self-assessment rubric to evaluate your participation in the discussion.

• In the story, the main conflict is _____.

• In the text, Yvette says "_____" about her mother substitute teaching at her school.

   In other words, Yvette feels _____ because _____
   _____.

• At the end of Yvette's science class, Yvette's mother says "_____"

   The text says Yvette's reaction is "_____"

   In other words, Yvette feels _____ because her mother _____
   _____.

• Then the text says Yvette's mother feels "_____" because Yvette "_____
   _____."

   In other words, Yvette's mother feels _____ because _____
   _____.

• I think the conflict is _____'s fault because _____
   _____.

SELF-ASSESSMENT RUBRIC CA-CCSS: ELD.PI.8.1.Ex

	4 I did this well.	3 I did this pretty well.	2 I did this a little bit.	1 I did not do this.
I identified details in the text that told about the conflict.				
I identified details in the text that told about how the characters feel about the conflict.				
I used my own words to paraphrase details from the text.				
I used details from the text to support my ideas about who is to blame for the conflict.				

REREAD

Reread paragraphs 4–10 of "Mom's First Day." After you reread, complete the Using Language and Meaningful Interactions activities.

USING LANGUAGE   CA-CCSS: ELD.PI.8.8.Ex

Read each sentence from "Mom's First Day," and note the figurative language in bold. Then choose the meaning of the figurative language in each sentence.

1. Everybody **freezes**.

   ○ Everyone stands still.
   ○ Everyone is covered in ice.

2. I'm so humiliated, all I can do is **bury my face** in Katie's shoulder.

   ○ Yvette puts her face in a hole.
   ○ Yvette hides her face.

3. Her disappointment hits **like a tidal wave**.

   ○ Mom has very strong feelings.
   ○ Mom was hit by a large wave.

MEANINGFUL INTERACTIONS   CA-CCSS: ELD.PI.8.1.Ex

What has Yvette done to make her mother feel unwelcome? What should she have done to make her feel welcome? Work with a partner to practice sharing and discussing your opinion. Use the speaking frames to add relevant information and evidence from the text to support your opinion.

• Yvette made her mother feel unwelcome by . . .

• I think this makes her mother feel unwelcome because . . .

• My opinion is that Yvette should have . . .

• Evidence supporting my opinion is . . .

• Do you think that Yvette should have . . . ?

• I think you said . . .

• I agree / don't agree because . . .

IT'S NOT FAIR

English Language
Development

FICTION

INTRODUCTION

" It's Not Fair" is a retelling of the memorable episode from Mark Twain's *The Adventures of Tom Sawyer* in which Tom uses charm and ingenuity to trick others into doing chores for him. In this retelling, a girl named Cassie must plant her aunt's flower garden on the same day as the annual county fair. Cassie relies on her own cleverness—and a scheme learned from reading classic American literature—to trick her friends into doing the work.

"A satisfied smile crept across Cassie's face."

FIRST READ

1   Cassie imagined the taste of caramel apples and the feel of the wind in her hair at the top of the Ferris wheel. She could practically smell the freshly made popcorn and hear the sounds of children's laughter. Her despair deepened. It was bad enough that she got roped into planting her aunt's garden. Now she had to do it on the same day as the county fair. It wasn't fair. The path leading to the fairgrounds ran along her aunt's property. Cassie's friends would skip along this path on their way to a world of wonders she could only dream about, and she was certain they'd stop to ridicule her about how she had to work while they had the time of their lives at the fair. The mere thought of it was enough to make her wish she could bury her head in the dirt instead of the flower bulbs she was supposed to plant.

2   Cassie took up the **trowel** and started to dig. Bella Stevenson, the most popular girl in class and the person Cassie was dreading the most, **ambled** down the path. She was dragging a red wagon behind her, which was carrying an apple pie.

3   Cassie kept digging. A plan was forming in her brain. She remembered reading how Tom Sawyer convinced his friends to whitewash a fence for him. If she played the role perfectly, she could accomplish the same task.

4   "It's too bad you're stuck here while the rest of us get to have fun at the fair!" Bella called out.

5   "Fun? This is more fun than that silly fair. The same food and rides every year! Planting bulbs under the sweet spring sunshine? That's a **novelty**!"

6   "If it's that much fun, it's not fair that you keep it all to yourself."

7   A satisfied smile crept across Cassie's face. Her plan had worked.

8   "I don't know. Aunt Lucy entrusted this job to me. I can't let just anyone do it. Tell you what. I'll trade you a few **bulbs** for some of that pie you made."

9   Bella was planning on entering the pie in the contest at the fair, but she didn't want to miss this chance. She accepted, handing Cassie a slice of pie and taking the trowel in exchange.

10 When Bella had grown tired, Penelope Winters strolled by. Cassie pulled the trick on her—this time trading the trowel for Penelope's sunglasses. By the end of the afternoon, Cassie had Bella's pie, Penelope's sunglasses, Randy's harmonica, Betty's kite, and Clark's bag of marbles.

11 Cassie was amazed at her classmates' **gullibility** and her own good fortune. "Tom Sawyer was right," she thought, "All you have to do to make somebody want something is make it seem hard to get."

 USING LANGUAGE   CA-CCSS: ELD.PI.8.6.c.Ex

Read each quotation and think about the meaning of the word in bold. Then choose the context clue that helped you determine the meaning of the word.

1. . . . the mere thought of it was enough to make her wish she could bury her head in the dirt instead of the flower **bulbs** she was supposed to plant.

    ○ flower
    ○ wish

2. Cassie took up the **trowel** and started to dig.

    ○ took up
    ○ to dig

3. Bella Stevenson, the most popular girl in class and the person Cassie was dreading the most, **ambled** down the path.

    ○ popular girl
    ○ down the path

4. Cassie pulled the trick on her — this time trading the trowel for Penelope's sunglasses. . . . Cassie was amazed at her classmates' **gullibility** and her own good fortune.

    ○ good fortune
    ○ pulled the trick

MEANINGFUL INTERACTIONS CA-CCSS: ELD.PI.8.1.Ex

Before you start your discussion, set turn-taking rules for the group.

1. _____

2. _____

3. _____

4. _____

5. _____

Use these questions to discuss your first impressions of "It's Not Fair":

- What is Cassie's problem?

- How does she solve her problem?

- Do you think Cassie's solution is clever or unfair? Why?

Work in small groups to practice taking turns speaking and listening during a discussion. Use the speaking frames to support your discussion. Then, use the self-assessment rubric to evaluate your participation in the discussion.

- Cassie's problem is . . .

- Cassie solves her problem by . . .

- In my opinion, Cassie's solution is . . . because . . .

- What evidence do you base your opinion on? Is it . . . ?

- I think you said . . . I agree / disagree because . . .

SELF-ASSESSMENT RUBRIC CA-CCSS: ELD.PI.8.1.Ex

	4 I did this well.	3 I did this pretty well.	2 I did this a little bit.	1 I did not do this.
I expressed my opinion clearly.				
I listened carefully to others' opinions.				
I waited my turn before speaking.				
I responded thoughtfully to my group members' ideas.				

REREAD

Reread paragraphs 1–3 of "It's Not Fair." After you reread, complete the Using Language and Meaningful Interactions activities.

USING LANGUAGE CA-CCSS: ELD.PI.8.8.Ex

Read the first draft of each sentence from the text and note the bold word or phrase. Then read the final draft of the text and consider the change the author made in bold. Then complete the chart by choosing the correct option for how the author's word choice helps readers understand.

Helps readers understand... Options		
how Cassie feels about Bella how great the fair is	how much fun Cassie's friends had how carefree the other children are	how strongly Cassie feels

First Draft	Final Draft	Helps readers understand...
Her **sadness** deepened.	Her **despair** deepened.	
Cassie's friends would **walk** along this path on their way to the fair...	Cassie's friends would **skip** along this path on their way to a world of wonders she could only dream about...	
Cassie's friends would travel along this path on their way to **the fair**...	Cassie's friends would skip along this path on their way to **a world of wonders she could only dream about**...	
... she was certain they'd stop to ridicule her about how she had to work while they had **fun** at the fair...	...she was certain they'd stop to ridicule her about how she had to work while they had **the time of their lives** at the fair...	
Bella Stevenson, **a girl from Cassie's class**, ambled down the path.	Bella Stevenson, **the most popular girl in class and the person Cassie was dreading the most**, ambled down the path.	

Please note that excerpts and passages in the StudySync® library and this workbook are intended as touchstones to generate interest in an author's work. The excerpts and passages do not substitute for the reading of entire texts, and StudySync® strongly recommends that students seek out and purchase the whole literary or informational work in order to experience it as the author intended. Links to online resellers are available in our digital library. In addition, complete works may be ordered through an authorized reseller by filling out and returning to StudySync® the order form enclosed in this workbook.

Reading & Writing Companion

89

MEANINGFUL INTERACTIONS CA-CCSS: ELD.PI.8.1.Ex

Based on what you have read in "It's Not Fair," what do you think the conflict suggests about human nature? Would you try to resolve the conflict in the same way as Cassie? Why or why not? Work in small groups to practice sharing and discussing your opinions, using the speaking frames. Then, use the self-assessment rubric to evaluate your participation in the discussion.

- I would / would not resolve the conflict in the same way as Cassie because . . .

- In my opinion, the conflict shows that humans are . . . because . . .

- I think . . . said that . . .

- I agree / don't agree with . . . that . . .

SELF-ASSESSMENT RUBRIC CA-CCSS: ELD.PI.8.1.Ex

	4 I did this well.	3 I did this pretty well.	2 I did this a little bit.	1 I did not do this.
I expressed my opinion clearly.				
I listened carefully to others' opinions.				
I spoke respectfully when disagreeing with others.				
I was courteous when persuading others to share my view.				

REREAD

Reread paragraphs 4–11 of "It's Not Fair." After you reread, complete the Using Language and Meaningful Interactions activities.

⚙ USING LANGUAGE CA-CCSS: ELD.PII.8.4.Ex

Complete the sentences by filling in the blanks.

1. Find the sentence in paragraph 5 that shows a comparison Cassie makes.

   This is more fun than that _____.

2. Find the sentence in paragraph 5 that shows what Cassie pretends to think about the fair.

   The _____ and _____ every year!

3. Find the sentence in paragraph 7 that shows how Cassie reacts when Bella falls for her trick.

   A _____ crept across Cassie's face.

4. Find the sentence in paragraph 8 that shows what Cassie wants to trade.

   I'll trade you a _____ for some of _____ you made.

5. Find the sentence in paragraph 10 that shows what Cassie is doing to her friends.

   Cassie pulled _____ on her—this time trading the trowel for Penelope's sunglasses.

6. Find the sentence in paragraph 11 that shows what Cassie thinks about her classmates and the results of her plan.

   Cassie was amazed at her _____ and her own _____.

Please note that excerpts and passages in the StudySync® library and this workbook are intended as touchstones to generate interest in an author's work. The excerpts and passages do not substitute for the reading of entire texts, and StudySync® strongly recommends that students seek out and purchase the whole literary or informational work in order to experience it as the author intended. Links to online resellers are available in our digital library. In addition, complete works may be ordered through an authorized reseller by filling out and returning to StudySync® the order form enclosed in this workbook.

Reading & Writing Companion

91

MEANINGFUL INTERACTIONS CA-CCSS: ELD.PI.8.1.Ex

What do you think of Cassie and the way she treats her classmates? What evidence from the text supports your opinion? Work with a partner to practice sharing and discussing your opinions, using the writing and speaking frames.

- My opinion is that the way Cassie treats her classmates is _____

  because _____

  _____ .

- The evidence I used to form my opinion is _____

  _____ .

- I think you said that . . . , but the text says . . .

- Why do you think that . . . ?

- I agree / disagree with your opinion because . . .

Reading & Writing Companion

ASSIGNMENTS   REVIEW   BINDER   BLASTS   LIBRARY

studysync

WRITE

EXTENDED WRITING PROJECT

Extended Writing Project Prompt and Directions:
As the selections you have read in this unit show, people make choices, some of which are m_____ experiences. People make choices, some of which are m_____ grow from their experiences. Choose two selections from _____ character or the narrator in each one. What does the mai_____ and how do the characters' experiences shape or even ch_____ analysis that shows how personal experience can change p_____ for worse.

Your literary analysis should include:
- an introduction that states a claim, or an opinion, about the theme or other aspects of one or more literary works.
- body paragraphs with relevant evidence from a literary text or texts that support the claim or opinion.
- a conclusion paragraph that follows from the body of the essay and effectively wraps up your analysis.

EXTENDED WRITING PROJECT
LITERARY ANALYSIS

Extended Writing Project:
Literary Analysis
by StudySync

1   WRITE

Font   Size   **B** *I* L U

EXTENDED
WRITING
PROJECT

LITERARY ANALYSIS

WRITING PROMPT

As the selections you have read in this unit show, people are shaped by their individual life experiences. People make choices, some of which are mistakes, but they often learn and grow from their experiences. Choose two selections from this unit and think about the main character or the narrator in each one. What does the main character or narrator value most, and how do the characters' experiences shape or even change their values? Write a literary analysis that shows how personal experience can change people for better or sometimes for worse.

Your literary analysis should include:

- an introduction that states a claim, or an opinion, about the theme or other aspects of one or more literary works.
- body paragraphs with relevant evidence from a literary text or texts that support the claim or opinion.
- a conclusion paragraph that follows from the body of the essay and effectively wraps up your analysis.

A **literary analysis** presents a writer's personal understanding or evaluation of a work of literature and then provides textual evidence—details, descriptions, and quotations—to support the evaluation. As with any evaluation, a literary analysis requires a writer to examine different parts of a work of literature in order to better understand and appreciate the work as a whole. It may discuss how the various elements of an individual work—such as setting, characters, and plot events—relate to each other. It might also analyze how two separate literary works handle similar themes and ideas.

Literary analysis is a form of argumentative writing. The writer makes a claim about one or more works of literature, and then provides evidence to support the claim. A strong literary analysis begins with a sound thesis statement that clearly expresses the writer's opinion or claim about some part of the work. After introducing the claim, the writer develops his or her ideas in the body of the text. Like all good essays, a literary analysis develops and supports the thesis with text evidence, and connects the ideas together with clear and specific transitions. These help readers to understand the logic behind the argument, and identify how well it is supported. The piece ends with a conclusion that clearly restates the main idea and shows that the analysis is sound and well-supported. The features of a literary analysis include:

- a clear thesis statement expressing the author's claim, or opinion, about the work
- an organizational structure with clear transitions that logically moves the reader through each step of the argument
- text evidence that supports the argument, in the form of quotations and other details from the text or texts
- precise language
- a conclusion that summarizes the author's position

You will receive more instructions and practice to help you create each of the elements that make up a literary analysis as you continue with this Extended Writing Project.

 ## STUDENT MODEL

Before you begin your own literary analysis, start by reading this essay. This is one student's response to the writing prompt. Be sure to highlight and annotate the features of a literary analysis that the student included as you read the essay.

Personal Experiences: The Pathway to Values

How do you define your own personal values? Are they the ideas that you feel are most important in life, the foundation for your every action and belief? Many people believe personal values form the core of a person's being, shaping our individual personalities as well as our decisions about what is right and wrong. But where do values come from? Many works of literature reveal how personal experiences can shape or even change a character's values. Mark Twain shows how this can occur in The Adventures of Tom Sawyer. *Judith Ortiz Cofer also illustrates this process in her short story, "Abuela Invents the Zero." Even though their main characters exist many years apart, and have very different lives, both*

Please note that excerpts and passages in the StudySync® library and this workbook are intended as touchstones to generate interest in an author's work. The excerpts and passages do not substitute for the reading of entire texts, and StudySync® strongly recommends that students seek out and purchase the whole literary or informational work in order to experience it as the author intended. Links to online resellers are available in our digital library. In addition, complete works may be ordered through an authorized reseller by filling out and returning to StudySync® the order form enclosed in this workbook.

Reading & Writing Companion   **95**

Twain and Ortiz Cofer show how personal experiences can shape a person's values for a lifetime.

Both Twain and Cofer Ortiz put characters into situations that reveal their personal values. In an excerpt from *The Adventures of Tom Sawyer*, readers find the main character painting a fence. The narrator relates how unhappy Tom is with the job. In the first paragraph of the excerpt, Tom "began to think of the fun he had planned for this day, and his sorrows multiplied" (Twain). This shows that Tom values fun more than the hard work of painting the fence. In Ortiz Cofer's short story, the author makes Constancia's values very clear. This teen-aged girl values her identity and standing in her American neighborhood far more than she values her family's Puerto Rican heritage and her grandmother's feelings. One illustration of this is when Constancia describes her embarrassment at being with her grandmother in public: "I try to walk far behind them in public so that no one will think we are together" (Ortiz Cofer).

Like every other human being, Tom Sawyer's and Constancia's values have been shaped by their personal experiences. Twain's Tom Sawyer has had experiences that lead him to value fun more than work as well as to value the opinions of his friends. This is shown when the narrator describes his thoughts: ". . . and they would make a world of fun of him for having to work—the very thought burnt him like fire" (Twain). The narrator even describes how Tom thinks about bribing his friends to do his work for him. He rejects the idea because he does not have enough valuables to trade for his freedom. Like Tom Sawyer, Ortiz Cofer's character's values are also shaped by her experiences. Constancia, the main character, is a teen-aged girl whose family has come to the United States from Puerto Rico. Her mother recalls the difficulty of her early life in Puerto Rico. She tells Constancia about how her grandmother "worked night and day to support them after their father died of a heart attack" (Ortiz Cofer). Constancia's mother values her mother's efforts and wants to make sure that Abuela's visit is fun for her. However, Constancia has not had the same experiences with Abuela. She has only met her a few times and does not feel close to her. She does not value Abuela in the same way her mother does. This is demonstrated by her behavior in the story. For example, when Constancia is forced to take her grandmother to church, she describes going into the building: ". . . Then I lead her down the aisle so that everybody can see me with my bizarre grandmother" (Ortiz Cofer).

Twain and Ortiz Cofer describe brief moments in their characters' lives, but even these small events influence the characters' values. In the case of Tom Sawyer, his values are confirmed and supported. He comes up with a scheme to get the other boys to do the painting for him. He does this by convincing them that the chore of painting the fence is not actually work at all, but rather great fun. The other boys happily part with their treasures in return for a turn with the paintbrush, and Tom learns that he can manipulate others to get the things he values, namely, free time and fun. Twain's narrator notes, "Tom said to himself that it was not such a hollow world, after all. He had discovered a great law of human action, without knowing it—namely, that in order to make a man or a boy covet a thing, it is only necessary to make the thing difficult to attain" (Twain). Constancia, on the other hand, suffers through her embarrassing moments with her grandmother only to discover that her feelings are not the only ones that mattered. Her grandmother was made to feel "like a zero, like a nothing" (Ortiz Cofer). Constancia's mother reminded her that the grandmother deserved more respect, because "if it wasn't for the old woman whose existence you don't seem to value, you and I would not be here" (Ortiz Cofer). As a result, Constancia's values begin to change. As she describes her thoughts, she notes "I think I understand how I made Abuela feel" and ". . . it's not easy to admit you've been a jerk" (Ortiz Cofer). These revelations show that Constancia's values were changing because of her experiences.

In both selections, the authors show how personal experiences shaped the values of the main characters. The importance Tom Sawyer placed on fun is only reinforced by the events in the story. He may have turned work into fun for others, but that was not his aim. Conversely, Constancia's personal values, and how she felt about her heritage and her grandmother, were shaken and perhaps changed now that she understands how her grandmother feels. Tom Sawyer's values arguably changed for the worse, but Constancia's values improved as she learned more about her *Abuela*. In these excerpts, both authors show how personal experiences and the responses of other people shape and mold everyone's values every day.

Please note that excerpts and passages in the StudySync® library and this workbook are intended as touchstones to generate interest in an author's work. The excerpts and passages do not substitute for the reading of entire texts, and StudySync® strongly recommends that students seek out and purchase the whole literary or informational work in order to experience it as the author intended. Links to online resellers are available in our digital library. In addition, complete works may be ordered through an authorized reseller by filling out and returning to StudySync® the order form enclosed in this workbook.

Reading & Writing Companion   97

THINK QUESTIONS

1. What is the claim or central idea of this essay?

2. How does the author of the Student Model support the claim or central idea?

3. How does the author show a connection between the character development in the selections and the development of values in real life? Support your answer with textual evidence from the essay.

4. Consider the prompt that will guide your writing project. Which selections or other resources could you use to write your own literary analysis? What ideas will you include in your piece?

5. Based on what you have read, listened to, or researched, how would you answer the following questions: *How can personal experiences impact values? How do values change based on experiences?* Provide some details that helped inform your answers.

PREWRITE

CA-CCSS: CA.RI.8.1, CA.W.8.5, CA.W.8.6, CA.W.8.9a

WRITING PROMPT

As the selections you have read in this unit show, people are shaped by their individual life experiences. People make choices, some of which are mistakes, but they often learn and grow from their experiences. Choose two selections from this unit and think about the main character or the narrator in each one. What does the main character or narrator value most, and how do the characters' experiences shape or even change their values? Write a literary analysis that shows how personal experience can change people for better or sometimes for worse.

Your literary analysis should include:

- an introduction that states a claim, or an opinion, about the theme or other aspects of one or more literary works.
- body paragraphs with relevant evidence from a literary text or texts that support the claim or opinion.
- a conclusion paragraph that follows from the body of the essay and effectively wraps up your analysis.

You have been reading and learning from selections that feature a cross-section of characters learning more about themselves and others through personal experiences. Now you will analyze these selections and use the information to write your own essay about how personal experiences can shape the values of individuals.

As you prepare to write your literary analysis in response to the Extended Writing Prompt above, consider the following questions for each of the selections you will use as the basis for your literary analysis:

- Which selections from the unit are you choosing to write about?

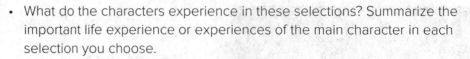

- What do the characters experience in these selections? Summarize the important life experience or experiences of the main character in each selection you choose.
- Are the experiences short, specific and limited, or will they have an impact that will last a lifetime?
- How does the author show what kind of impact the experience had on the character's values?
- Does the experience change the character for better or for worse?
- What predictions can you make about the future behavior of the character, based on the information given in the selection?
- How do you think this character's values will be challenged or reinforced as his or her life experiences continue?

Make a list of the answers to these questions for the characters in the selections you have chosen as the basis for your literary analysis. Do you see any patterns? Do you find any ideas that surface again and again? Looking for patterns and similarities that may emerge in more than one selection can help you solidify the ideas you want to discuss in your essay. Use this model to help you get started with your own prewriting:

Text: *The Adventures of Tom Sawyer* by Mark Twain

Character Experience: Tom Sawyer wished that he didn't have to work at whitewashing his aunt's fence, and he was envious of the "free" boys who passed by, all of whom were planning "delicious expeditions." By pretending that his work was more enjoyable and engaging than any game or adventure— and that only he was skilled enough to do it correctly—Tom convinced the boys to give him their treasures for a chance to join him and experience the "fun" of whitewashing.

How It Shaped the Character's Values: Tom learned that people will work hard if they don't feel that they are obliged to do it, and that "in order to make a man or boy covet a thing, it is only necessary to make the thing difficult to attain." The great value Tom once placed on "freedom" was lessened by his new understanding of the "great law of human action" he discovered through experience.

SKILL:
THESIS
STATEMENT

⭐ DEFINE

Literary analysis is a form of argumentative writing, and the focal point of argumentative writing is the thesis statement. This is a single sentence that summarizes the central or main idea of an essay by introducing the writer's claim about the essay topic. This is the claim that the writer will develop in the body of the essay and support with organized facts, details, quotations, definitions and other pieces of textual evidence. The thesis statement most often appears as the last sentence in the introductory paragraph of an essay.

⋯ IDENTIFICATION AND APPLICATION

- To identify the thesis statement in a passage:
  › Look at the last sentence of the introductory paragraph.
  › Find a sentence that makes a claim about the selection or selections.
  › Find a sentence that connects literary elements (like plot, style, imagery, structure, theme, or symbolism). It may also connect a literary element with real life.

- To evaluate the thesis statement in a passage:
  › Determine the author's claim.
  › Look for strong verbs (action verbs instead of verbs of being).
  › Look for clear and specific transitions that clearly show the relationship between ideas.
  › Determine if each of the passage's main ideas support the thesis in a logical manner.

MODEL

The following paragraph is the introduction from the student model literary analysis "Personal Experiences: The Pathway to Values":

How do you define your own personal values? Are they the ideas that you feel are most important in life, the foundation for your every action and belief? Many people believe personal values form the core of a person's being, shaping our individual personalities as well as our decisions about what is right and wrong. But where do values come from? Many works of literature reveal how personal experiences can shape or even change a character's values. Mark Twain shows how this can occur in *The Adventures of Tom Sawyer*. Judith Ortiz Cofer also illustrates this process in her short story, "Abuela Invents the Zero." **Even though their main characters exist many years apart, and have very different lives, both Twain and Ortiz Cofer show how personal experiences can shape a person's values for a lifetime.**

Notice the boldfaced claim at the end of the paragraph. This student's claim responds to the prompt, by addressing how two authors, Mark Twain and Julia Cofer Ortiz, show how personal experiences can shape a person's values for a lifetime. It also expresses the writer's opinion: even though the main characters live in two totally different time periods, the power of personal experience transcends, or goes beyond, these differences.

 ## PRACTICE

Write a thesis statement for your literary analysis that clearly states the central claim or idea that you will address in your essay. When you are finished, trade with a partner and give feedback to one another. Consider these questions: Does this statement express a clear claim? Does this statement make the focus of the essay obvious? Does this statement specifically address the prompt for this assignment? Give suggestions to your partner that will help him or her strengthen the thesis statement, and remember to keep your suggestions kind and constructive.

SKILL:
ORGANIZE
ARGUMENTATIVE
WRITING

⭐ DEFINE

A literary analysis is a type of argumentative essay. It is intended to convince readers of an author's position or point of view on a subject that is related to one or more pieces of literature. Authors state their claim, or argument, in a thesis statement. Then they support that claim with valid reasoning and logical, relevant evidence from reliable sources. To do so, the author must organize and present the reasons and relevant evidence—the details and quotations from the text or texts—in a logical and convincing way. The writer must select an organizational structure that best suits the argument.

The writer of a literary analysis can choose from a number of organizational structures, including compare and contrast, sequential order, problem and solution, cause and effect, and chronological order.

••• IDENTIFICATION AND APPLICATION

- When selecting an organizational structure for a piece of writing, writers consider the connections between most of the information they are writing about. They ask themselves these questions:

  › To support my idea, will I compare and contrast ideas or details in the text?

  › Will I raise a question or identify a problem in my argument? Do I have supporting evidence that suggests a solution or an answer?

  › Does most of my supporting evidence suggest a cause and effect relationship?

  › To support my claim, does it make sense to retell the events from the text or texts in sequential order?

- Writers often use specific cue words and phrases to help readers recognize the organizational structure of their writing:

  › Compare and contrast: *like, unlike, and, both, similar to, different from, while, but, conversely, although, also*

Please note that excerpts and passages in the StudySync® library and this workbook are intended as touchstones to generate interest in an author's work. The excerpts and passages do not substitute for the reading of entire texts, and StudySync® strongly recommends that students seek out and purchase the whole literary or informational work in order to experience it as the author intended. Links to online resellers are available in our digital library. In addition, complete works may be ordered through an authorized reseller by filling out and returning to StudySync® the order form enclosed in this workbook.

Reading & Writing Companion   **103**

> › Order of importance: *most, most important, least, least important, first, finally, mainly, to begin with*
> › Problem and solution: *consequently, so,* and *as a result* can signal a solution
> › Cause-effect: *because, as a consequence of, as a result, cause, effect, so*
> › Sequential order: *first, next, then, second, finally*

- The writer develops an opinion or point of view on the topic and states a claim.
- The claim is stated in a thesis statement and is supported by logical reasoning.
- Text evidence is factual information from the text that supports the author's claim. In a literary analysis this would include examples and quotations from the texts that support the claim and do not include bias or personal opinions.
- A restatement of the claim is found in the concluding paragraph.

 MODEL

Organization is a critical part of crafting a convincing literary analysis or other type of argumentative essay. The essay's organization leads the reader from the claim made in the introductory paragraph, through a series of main ideas with supporting details that are designed to build a body of evidence that will persuade the reader. The concluding paragraph should restate the thesis and make all of the connections clear. Read through these paragraphs from the Student Model once again, and pay special attention to the organizational structure used by the author.

Personal Experiences: The Pathway to Values

How do you define your own personal values? Are they the ideas that you feel are most important in life, the foundation for your every action and belief? Many people believe personal values form the core of a person's being, shaping our individual personalities as well as our decisions about what is right and wrong. But where do values come from? Many works of literature reveal how personal experiences can shape or even change a character's values. Mark Twain shows how this can occur in The Adventures of Tom Sawyer. Judith Ortiz Cofer also illustrates this process in her short story, "Abuela Invents the Zero." **Even though their main characters exist**

many years apart, and have very different lives, both Twain and Ortiz Cofer show how personal experiences can shape a person's values for a lifetime.

Both Twain and Ortiz Cofer put characters into situations that reveal their personal values. In an excerpt from *The Adventures of Tom Sawyer*, readers find the main character painting a fence. The narrator relates how unhappy Tom is with the job. In the first paragraph of the excerpt, Tom "began to think of the fun he had planned for this day, and his sorrows multiplied" (Twain). This shows that Tom values fun more than the hard work of painting the fence. In Ortiz Cofer's short story, the author makes Constancia's values very clear. This teen-aged girl values her identity and standing in her American neighborhood far more than she values her family's Puerto Rican heritage and her grandmother's feelings. One illustration of this is when Constancia describes her embarrassment at being with her grandmother in public: "I try to walk far behind them in public so that no one will think we are together" (Ortiz Cofer).

The author used a chart to organize the information he had brainstormed in earlier lessons.

Character	Initial Value(s)	Experiences	Ending Value(s)
Tom Sawyer	Values fun and freedom	• Had to paint fence • Tried to get others to do his work • Successfully convinced other boys to work by telling them it was fun	Values of fun and freedom strengthened; learned how to manipulate others

Please note that excerpts and passages in the StudySync® library and this workbook are intended as touchstones to generate interest in an author's work. The excerpts and passages do not substitute for the reading of entire texts, and StudySync® strongly recommends that students seek out and purchase the whole literary or informational work in order to experience it as the author intended. Links to online resellers are available in our digital library. In addition, complete works may be ordered through an authorized reseller by filling out and returning to StudySync® the order form enclosed in this workbook.

Reading & Writing Companion 105

Character	Initial Value(s)	Experiences	Ending Value(s)
Constancia	Values social standing, being like her peers, and her own feelings	• Had to escort grandmother • Was embarrassed by grandmother's clothing • Was embarrassed by grandmother getting lost • Got into trouble with parents • Made her grandmother feel bad	Reconsiders values of family and respect for elders, changes from valuing self, peers and social standing alone to including family, tradition, and elders

The introductory paragraph contains the following thesis statement: "Even though their main characters exist many years apart, and have very different lives, both Twain and Ortiz Cofer show how personal experiences can shape a person's values for a lifetime." This statement makes a clear claim that the two authors use their characters to show how personal experiences influence values. In the second paragraph, the author claims that "Both Twain and Ortiz Cofer put characters into situations that reveal their personal values." The author is using a compare and contrast organizational pattern here, with the clue word "both" indicating the similarities that exist between the characters created by Mark Twain and Julia Ortiz Cofer.

 PRACTICE

Using either the *Compare and Contrast Literary Analysis Graphic Organizer,* the *Cause and Effect Literary Analysis Graphic Organizer,* or another organizer of your choosing, gather information about the main characters in the texts you will be analyzing and use that information to determine an appropriate organizational structure for your literary analysis. As possible, you should include ideas that emerged during the prewriting exercise. Ask yourself: Based on the information I collected in the organizer, does the text structure I initially chose work well, or would some other structure be more effective? Exchange your chart with a partner and offer each other feedback.

Copyright © BookheadEd Learning, LLC

SKILL: SUPPORTING DETAILS

⭐ DEFINE

In argumentative writing, writers develop their main idea with relevant evidence called **supporting details.** These details can include any fact, definition, concrete information, example, or quotation that helps to prove the author's claim and is closely related to the thesis statement, or main idea. Relevant supporting details are the key to the success of a writer's argument. It makes the argument more convincing and persuasive to the reader, helps develop the ideas the author presents, and clarifies the writer's understanding and interpretation of the text. Without reasons and relevant evidence, the writer would simply be stating his or her opinion about a theme or a central idea.

••• IDENTIFICATION AND APPLICATION

Step 1:

Review your thesis statement. To identify relevant supporting details, ask this question: What is the claim I am making about this topic? Here is the thesis statement from the student model, "Personal Experiences: The Pathway to Values":

> **Even though their main characters exist many years apart and have very different lives, both Mark Twain and Julia Ortiz Cofer show how personal experiences can shape one's values for a lifetime.**

What claim is the author making? The author is saying that both Mark Twain and Julia Ortiz Cofer demonstrate through their characters in *The Adventures of Tom Sawyer* and "Abuela Invents the Zero" that personal experiences influence a person's values.

Step 2:

Ask what a reader needs to know about the topic, or claim, in order to understand it. To understand the thesis statement of this analysis, a reader

Please note that excerpts and passages in the StudySync® library and this workbook are intended as touchstones to generate interest in an author's work. The excerpts and passages do not substitute for the reading of entire texts, and StudySync® strongly recommends that students seek out and purchase the whole literary or informational work in order to experience it as the author intended. Links to online resellers are available in our digital library. In addition, complete works may be ordered through an authorized reseller by filling out and returning to StudySync® the order form enclosed in this workbook.

Reading & Writing Companion 107

must first know what values the characters have at the beginning of their respective tales. The writer explains how Mark Twain reveals Tom's initial values in *The Adventures of Tom Sawyer:*

> In the first paragraph of the excerpt, Tom *"began to think of the fun he had planned for this day, and his sorrows multiplied"* (Twain). This shows that Tom values fun more than the hard work of painting the fence.

He then supplies additional details to show how Ortiz Cofer reveals Constancia's initial values:

> This teen-aged girl values her identity and standing in her American neighborhood far more than she values her family's Puerto Rican heritage and her grandmother's feelings. One illustration of this is when Constancia describes her embarrassment at being with her grandmother in public: *"I try to walk far behind them in public so that no one will think we are together"* (Ortiz Cofer).

Step 3:

Search for facts, quotations, research, and the conclusions of others to help strengthen and support your thesis statement. As you search for details, carefully evaluate their relevance to your main idea. Ask yourself:

- Is this information necessary to the reader's understanding of the topic?
- Does this information help to develop and support my claim?
- Does this information relate closely to my thesis? Is it taken directly from the texts I am analyzing?
- Can I find better evidence that will provide stronger support for my point?

 MODEL

Read the following excerpt from the student model essay, "Personal Experiences: The Pathway to Values":

> **Twain and Ortiz Cofer describe brief moments in their characters' lives, but even these small events influence the characters' values.** In the case of Tom Sawyer, his values are confirmed and supported. He comes up with a scheme to get the other boys to do the painting for him. He does this by convincing them that the chore of painting the fence is not actually work at all, but rather great fun. The other boys happily part with their treasures in return

for a turn with the paintbrush, and Tom learns that he can manipulate others to get the things he values, namely, free time and fun. **Twain's narrator notes, "Tom said to himself that it was not such a hollow world, after all. He had discovered a great law of human action, without knowing it—namely, that in order to make a man or a boy covet a thing, it is only necessary to make the thing difficult to attain"** (Twain). Constancia, on the other hand, suffers through her embarrassing moments with her grandmother only to discover that her feelings are not the only ones that mattered. Her grandmother was made to feel "like a zero, like a nothing" (Ortiz Cofer). Constancia's mother reminded her that the grandmother deserved more respect, because "if it wasn't for the old woman whose existence you don't seem to value, you and I would not be here" (Cofer Ortiz). As a result, Constancia's values begin to change. **As she describes her thoughts, she notes "I think I understand how I made Abuela feel" and ". . . it's not easy to admit you've been a jerk"** (Ortiz Cofer). These revelations show that Constancia's values were changing because of her experiences.

Notice how the paragraph begins with the author's clear statement of a main idea that builds on the claim of the thesis: "Twain and Ortiz Cofer describe brief moments in their characters' lives, but even these small events influence the characters' values." Next, the author pulls supporting evidence from Twain's passage about Tom Sawyer, describing how Tom manipulates the other boys into doing his work. This evidence is quoted directly from the text. Then the author includes supporting evidence from Ortiz Cofer's story, citing the change in Constancia. These examples provide strong supporting evidence that the snippets of experience described in both texts affected the characters' values.

The author includes evidence about both characters in the paragraph, setting up a contrast between them that is in keeping with the essay's compare and contrast organizational structure. The supporting evidence includes quotations from both authors' works, adding strength to the analysis and reinforcing the writer's original claim that personal experiences influence values.

 PRACTICE

Write a paragraph for your literary analysis that supports a claim or main idea in that paragraph as well as your overall thesis by drawing relevant evidence from one or more of the unit texts. Be sure to include an explanation of how the evidence supports the claim you are trying to make. Exchange your paragraphs with a partner and provide each other feedback. Remember that you can use this paragraph or a revised version in later stages of the writing process.

Please note that excerpts and passages in the StudySync® library and this workbook are intended as touchstones to generate interest in an author's work. The excerpts and passages do not substitute for the reading of entire texts, and StudySync® strongly recommends that students seek out and purchase the whole literary or informational work in order to experience it as the author intended. Links to online resellers are available in our digital library. In addition, complete works may be ordered through an authorized reseller by filling out and returning to StudySync® the order form enclosed in this workbook.

Reading & Writing Companion   **109**

PLAN

CA-CCSS: CA.W.8.1a, CA.W.8.1b, CA.W.8.4, CA.W.8.5, CA.W.8.6, CA.W.8.9a, CA.W.8.10, CA.SL.8.1a, CA.SL.8.1b, CA.SL.8.1c, CA.SL.8.1d

WRITING PROMPT

As the selections you have read in this unit show, people are shaped by their individual life experiences. People make choices, some of which are mistakes, but they often learn and grow from their experiences. Choose two selections from this unit and think about the main character or the narrator in each one. What does the main character or narrator value most, and how do the characters' experiences shape or even change their values? Write a literary analysis that shows how personal experience can change people for better or sometimes for worse.

Your literary analysis should include:

- an introduction that states a claim, or an opinion, about the theme or other aspects of one or more literary works.
- body paragraphs with relevant evidence from a literary text or texts that support the claim or opinion.
- a conclusion paragraph that follows from the body of the essay and effectively wraps up your analysis.

You have been studying techniques that authors use to convey information, as well as examining selections that discuss the relationship between personal experiences and values. Now you will use these ideas to create your own literary analysis essay.

In previous lessons, you have created one or more graphic organizers containing information about different authors and how they have shown the connection between their characters' personal experiences and their personal values. You have created a thesis statement, considered audience and purpose, identified an organizational structure that would work best for

NOTES

your analysis, and drafted a body paragraph with a main idea supported by details drawn from one or more unit texts. Now it's time to create a roadmap that will help you put all of the pieces into place. It's time to plan your essay.

Consider and answer the following questions as you develop the roadmap to your essay:

- What can you tell about each character's values at the beginning of each selection?
- What personal experiences are related in each selection?
- What changes do you perceive in the characters' values at the conclusion of each selection?
- How did each of the characters' personal experiences impact his or her values?
- In what ways do you think these changes in values will impact the characters' future behavior or actions?
- What connection do you see between experiences and values in the lives of others and in your own life?

Now make a model to use in writing your own essay. You can follow this guide:

Literary Analysis Road Map

Introductory Paragraph

Interesting beginning or hook:

Introduction of sources:

Thesis Statement or Claim:

Body Paragraph 1 Topic:

Supporting Detail #1:

Supporting Detail #2:

Body Paragraph 2 Topic:

Supporting Detail #1:

Supporting Detail #2:

Please note that excerpts and passages in the StudySync® library and this workbook are intended as touchstones to generate interest in an author's work. The excerpts and passages do not substitute for the reading of entire texts, and StudySync® strongly recommends that students seek out and purchase the whole literary or informational work in order to experience it as the author intended. Links to online resellers are available in our digital library. In addition, complete works may be ordered through an authorized reseller by filling out and returning to StudySync® the order form enclosed in this workbook.

Reading & Writing Companion   111

Body Paragraph 3 Topic:

Supporting Detail #1:

Supporting Detail #2:

Closing Paragraph:

Powerful closing argument:

SKILL: INTRODUCTIONS

★ DEFINE

The introduction is the opening paragraph or section of a literary analysis or other nonfiction text. The introduction of a literary analysis identifies the texts or the topic to be discussed, states the writer's claim or thesis statement, and previews the supporting evidence that will appear in the body of the text. The introduction is also the place where most writers include a "hook" that is intended to connect with and engage readers.

••• IDENTIFICATION AND APPLICATION

- In a literary analysis, the introduction is where the writer identifies the texts and the topic to be discussed. Once readers have that information, they can concentrate on the writer's claim, which is expressed in the thesis statement.

- A literary analysis is a form of argument, so the writer's claim is an important part of the introduction. The claim is a direct statement that gives the writer's opinion or interpretation of some aspect of the texts under discussion. By stating the claim in the introduction, the writer lets readers know the ideas he or she will explore in the body of the analysis. Establishing a claim here also allows readers to form their own opinions, which they can then measure against the writer's as they read the literary analysis.

- Another use of the introduction is to provide a preview of the supporting evidence that will follow in the body of the text. By using the introduction to hint at key details, the writer can establish an effective argument, increasing the likelihood that readers will agree with his or her claim.

- Authors sometimes include counter arguments in a literary analysis or argumentative essay. A counter argument is an argument or set of reasons put forward to oppose an idea or theory developed in another argument. A counter argument can make an argument stronger. This is because it gives the writer the chance to respond to readers' possible

Please note that excerpts and passages in the StudySync® library and this workbook are intended as touchstones to generate interest in an author's work. The excerpts and passages do not substitute for the reading of entire texts, and StudySync® strongly recommends that students seek out and purchase the whole literary or informational work in order to experience it as the author intended. Links to online resellers are available in our digital library. In addition, complete works may be ordered through an authorized reseller by filling out and returning to StudySync® the order form enclosed in this workbook.

Reading & Writing Companion   113

objections before they have finished reading. It also shows that the writer is a reasonable person who has considered both sides of the debate. Both of these can make an essay more persuasive.

- A "hook" in the opening of an essay is something that grabs a reader and draws him or her in. In other words, a good hook engages readers' interest and makes them want to keep reading. A hook might be an intriguing image, a surprising detail or opinion, a funny anecdote, or a startling statistic. The hook should appeal to the audience and help readers connect to the topic in a meaningful way so that they will take the writer's claim seriously.

 ## MODEL

Read this introduction from "Point: Give Teens Some Work to Do! It's Good for Them and Everyone Else" from *Mandatory Volunteer Work for Teenagers*. Try to find all of the attributes of a strong introduction as you read.

> **Teenagers today live in a confusing world. The media sends many mixed messages about what it means to be a helpful person in society.** One of the best ways to help teens find their way is to **make volunteer work a mandatory part of their school curriculum.** Some people would immediately argue that this is an unnecessary action—many teens already volunteer without it being a requirement. It's true: teens have a propensity to volunteer more than adults. However, as a society we should make sure that not just some, but all, teens volunteer. Many of the teens that volunteer do so as part of a religious group or a youth leadership organization. In fact, 46 percent of teens who volunteer are working with a religious group or a youth leadership organization while only 18 percent of teens who volunteer are working with school-based groups. **This shows that clearly the best way to include all teens in the benefits of volunteering is to add mandatory volunteer work to the school curriculum.**

The author opens with the sentence, "Teenagers today live in a confusing world." What type of hook is used here? This author chose to capture readers' attention by stating a provocative opinion about the world of teens today. This opinion is engaging because most readers would agree with it. Teens themselves are likely to view their world as confusing and challenging, simply because, as they leave childhood behind, they find they have more responsibilities as well as decisions to make. Older readers may look at the increasing complexity of a world filled with gadgets, tests, and opportunities that weren't available to them at the same age, and so agree that today's world is confusing for teenagers. The author used that one sentence to grab the attention of a wide cross-section of readers.

The very next sentence, "The media sends many mixed messages about what it means to be a helpful person in society," shows that the topic is the center of a controversy. This is why readers might consider this information to be important, which provides the second characteristic of a strong introduction: giving readers a reason to read.

The writer then presents a counter argument: "Some people would immediately argue that this is an unnecessary action—many teens already volunteer without it being a requirement." While in agreement with the last part of this statement, the writer also presents statistics that show most teens do not volunteer as part of a school-based group, and mandatory volunteering in schools would make it possible for all teens to volunteer. The author, however, does not introduce sources for these statistics in this paragraph. The sources are listed at the end in a bibliography, but mentioning them here would strengthen and add credibility to the introduction.

The thesis statement for this essay is found in the last sentence of the paragraph, "This shows that clearly the best way to include all teens in the benefits of volunteering is to add mandatory volunteer work to the school curriculum." The author makes it very clear that the entire essay will be arguing in favor of adding mandatory volunteer requirements to students' coursework.

 PRACTICE

Write an introduction for your literary analysis that includes a hook to engage the reader's interest, some background information about your topic, an overview of your sources and a sound thesis statement that clearly states the central claim that you will prove in your essay. When you are finished, trade with a partner and give feedback to one another. Consider these questions: What hook did the author use to capture reader's interest? Was it effective? Why or why not? Does this introduction provide background information to orient the reader and give an overview of the sources? Is there a clear and strong thesis statement at the end of the paragraph? Give suggestions to your partner that will help him or her strengthen the introduction, and remember to keep your suggestions kind and constructive.

SKILL: CONCLUSIONS

 DEFINE

The conclusion is the final paragraph or section of a nonfiction text. In a literary analysis, the conclusion brings the writer's argument to a close. It follows directly from the claim made in the introduction and the reasons and relevant evidence provided in the body of the text. A conclusion should restate the thesis statement and summarize the central idea (or ideas) covered. In some kinds of writing, a conclusion might also include a recommendation or solution, a call to action, or a statement of insight. Many conclusions try to connect with readers by encouraging them to apply what they have learned from the text to their own lives.

IDENTIFICATION AND APPLICATION

- The conclusion of a literary analysis draws a clear line of reasoning between all of the author's supporting points back to the claim made in the thesis statement.

- A strong conclusion restates the thesis or author's claim and leaves no doubt in the reader's mind that the claim has been fully supported.

- The conclusion may also include some action for the reader to take, a recommendation, or some overall insight that the author wants to be sure the reader understands.

- The conclusion affects the reader's final impression of the essay, and so it must be strong in order to convince the reader that the claim has been completely proven.

MODEL

In the opening paragraph of the student model, "Personal Experiences: The Pathway to Values," the writer states the claim he will attempt to prove in his literary analysis:

Even though their main characters exist many years apart and have very different lives, both Twain and Julia Ortiz Cofer show how personal experiences can shape one's values for a lifetime.

Now, reread the conclusion from the student model. Look for the elements of a strong conclusion as you read.

In both selections, the authors show how personal experiences shaped the values of the main characters. The importance Tom Sawyer placed on fun is only reinforced by the events in the story. He may have turned work into fun for others, but that was not his aim. Conversely, Constancia's personal values, and how she felt about her heritage and her grandmother, were shaken and perhaps changed now that she understands how her grandmother feels. **Tom Sawyer's values arguably changed for the worse, but Constancia's values improved as she learned more about her *Abuela*. In these excerpts, both authors show how personal experiences and the responses of other people shape and mold everyone's values every day.**

First, notice how the author rephrased the claim from the thesis statement in the last sentence of the paragraph. Compare the closing sentence—"In these excerpts, both authors show how personal experiences and the responses of other people shape and mold everyone's values every day"— with the thesis statement shared earlier: "Even though their main characters exist many years apart and have very different lives, both Twain and Julia Ortiz Cofer show how personal experiences can shape one's values for a lifetime." The two sentences are not identical, but both include references to the authors and characters that were used as supporting details in the essay, and both include the claim that the author wanted to prove. The essay's conclusion connects back to the ideas in the introduction.

In the middle of the concluding paragraph, the author adds an additional insight for the reader to consider. The sentence, "Tom Sawyer's values arguably changed for the worse, but Constancia's values improved as she learned more about her *Abuela*," indicates that not only do experiences influence values, but also that values and the experiences that create them can be positive or negative.

Finally, the author of the student model devotes some effort in the conclusion to summarizing the main points of the essay. He reviews the experiences and their impact on the personal values of both characters, though this information was presented in greater detail earlier in the essay. This summary of the main points refreshes the reader's memory and highlights the important ideas that the author wanted to stress.

Copyright © BookheadEd Learning, LLC

This conclusion is a strong one because it restates the thesis statement, it summarizes the main ideas, it provides an additional insight, and it offers closure to the reader. The author of the student essay seems confident that he has proven his original claim and that the reader now believes that personal experiences shape values.

 PRACTICE

Write a conclusion for your literary analysis. When you have finished, trade with a partner and review each other's concluding paragraphs. Consider the following questions to help your partner improve his or her conclusion: "Did the author review the main supporting ideas of the argument for the essay's claim or thesis? Did the author offer any additional insight or a call to action? What is your overall impression of the conclusion? How could it be improved?" Remember to offer your suggestions in a positive, helpful manner.

NOTES

DRAFT

CA-CCSS: CA.W.8.1a, CA.W.8.1b, CA.W.8.1c. CA.W.8.1e, CA.W.8.4, CA.W.8.5, CA.W.8.6, CA.W.8.9a, CA.W.8.10, CA.SL.8.1a, CA.SL.8.1c, CA.L.8.1a, CA.L.8.6

WRITING PROMPT

As the selections you have read in this unit show, people are shaped by their individual life experiences. People make choices, some of which are mistakes, but they often learn and grow from their experiences. Choose two selections from this unit and think about the main character or the narrator in each one. What does the main character or narrator value most, and how do the characters' experiences shape or even change their values? Write a literary analysis that shows how personal experience can change people for better or sometimes for worse.

Your literary analysis should include:

- an introduction that states a claim, or an opinion, about the theme or other aspects of one or more literary works.

- body paragraphs with relevant evidence from a literary text or texts that support the claim or opinion.

- a conclusion paragraph that follows from the body of the essay and effectively wraps up your analysis.

You have generated many ideas for your literary analysis, chosen an organizational structure, created a thesis statement, gathered supporting information, and considered your audience and purpose. Look over all of the organizers and notes you have made from previous lessons. Think about the things you have learned about writing introductions and conclusions and including transitions. You can use these skills to mold all of the pieces into a strong essay.

Reread the writing prompt above. Do any new ideas come to mind? Incorporate these into the information you've already prepared. Use this opportunity to write the first draft of your essay.

When drafting, use these questions as a guide:

- How can I make the hook in my introduction more effective?
- How can I clarify my thesis statement to make my claim stronger?
- Which facts, details, quotations and supporting details best support my claim?
- In what way can I improve the organizational structure of my essay to create a more logical flow of ideas?
- How can I improve my use of transitions to better show the connections between ideas?
- Where can I use more precise language, such as academic or domain-specific words and phrases, or more vivid details to make my point?
- Have I used verbals, including gerunds, participles, and infinitives, correctly?
- How can I draw all of these ideas together to show that I have proven my claim?

It's time to write the draft of your essay. Use the lists, notes, graphic organizers, roadmaps, and paragraphs that you have already created in previous lessons. Remember to pay special attention to finalizing your thesis statement because a strong thesis statement is the first step to a strong analysis essay. Build your introductory paragraph and your body paragraphs. Use your closing paragraph to review the details you have included to support your claim and leave your readers with a lasting impression. Draw everything together so the reader can have no doubt that you have proven your claim. Before you submit your draft, reread it carefully. Be sure that you have addressed all of the aspects of the prompt.

SKILL: STYLE

 DEFINE

Style is how authors express their ideas and convey information through language. It is revealed through the author's choice of words and sentence construction. An author's style can be formal, suitable for academic or professional work, or informal, suitable for relaxed communication between family and friends. Before starting to write, an author must think about his or her purpose and audience and then tailor the language to suit both. Style also requires an awareness of the rules for writing standardized English. Tone is another element of style. In written composition, tone is the attitude a writer has toward a subject or an audience.

 IDENTIFICATION AND APPLICATION

- Style is the way the author uses words and constructs sentences. It also includes the tone, or the author's attitude toward the audience or the topic.

- Literary essays have a formal style. This means that the author uses third person, employs precise and/or specialized vocabulary suitable to the topic, varies the sentence structure, and avoids the use of slang.

- A formal style uses varied sentence structure. The writing does not sound choppy due to too many short, simple sentences. It also does not sound confusing because of too many long, complicated sentences.

- The tone of formal writing is respectful, thoughtful and serious.

- When using a formal style, a writer tries to choose words and phrases that mean exactly what he or she intends. The author avoids vague words and phrases such as "sometimes" or "in most cases" and instead substitutes specific words and figures, such as "in 75 percent of all cases" or "in each instance."

Please note that excerpts and passages in the StudySync® library and this workbook are intended as touchstones to generate interest in an author's work. The excerpts and passages do not substitute for the reading of entire texts, and StudySync® strongly recommends that students seek out and purchase the whole literary or informational work in order to experience it as the author intended. Links to online resellers are available in our digital library. In addition, complete works may be ordered through an authorized reseller by filling out and returning to StudySync® the order form enclosed in this workbook.

Reading & Writing Companion   **121**

- The author pays special attention to transitions, making them as clear and specific as possible. The transitions in formal writing should show the relationship between ideas, instead of simply stringing them together.

MODEL

The reading selection *Mandatory Volunteer Work for Teenagers* includes two essays. Although the authors express opposing positions on the central question of mandatory teen volunteering, both essays maintain a formal style. Read the two introductions to examine the elements of formal style.

Point: Give Teens Some Work to Do! It's Good for Them and Everyone Else

Teenagers today live in a confusing world. The media sends many mixed messages about what it means to be a helpful person in society. One of the best ways to help teens find their way is to make volunteer work a mandatory part of their school curriculum. Some people would immediately argue that this is an unnecessary action—many teens already volunteer without it being a requirement. It's true: teens have a propensity to volunteer more than adults. **However, as a society we should make sure that not just some, but all, teens volunteer.** Many of the teens that volunteer do so as part of a religious group or a youth leadership organization. In fact, 46 percent of teens who volunteer are working with a religious group or a youth leadership organization while only 18 percent of teens who volunteer are working with school-based groups. This shows that clearly the best way to include all teens in the benefits of volunteering is to add mandatory volunteer work to the school curriculum.

Counterpoint: Mandatory Volunteer Work Does More Harm Than Good

Most people agree that **teenagers** today live in a difficult world. **There are more pressures facing the modern teen than we can count: school, work, family, sports, and other extracurricular activities, just to name a few.** However, some people think that we should add to that load of pressures by making volunteer work a mandatory part of the school curriculum. One of the greatest arguments for this action is that mandatory volunteer work will prepare students for the future by giving them work experience, but the flaw in this logic is that many teens already gain work experience through paying jobs. In fact, many of the teens working paying jobs are doing so out of necessity—to pay for gas to get back and forth to school, or to help their families with extra money. Those teens without paying jobs still have plenty of prospects for gaining work experience in other ways such as an internship, or working at a school paper. Another argument for making volunteer work a mandatory part of school curriculum is that this work will help teens gain self-esteem and self-confidence. However, having time to socialize and develop hobbies and other interests is more important for self-esteem and self-confidence than volunteering.

What did you notice about the two introductions that indicates the authors' use of formal style? Let's begin with the language that the authors chose. Notice that neither author used any slang or informal words or phrases. Instead of using a phrase such as "kids today live in a crazy, kooky, mixed-up world" in the first paragraph, the author writes "teenagers today live in a confusing world." Both authors also used precise vocabulary in their introductions. They refer to "teenagers" as opposed to "young people" or "kids." Both authors also use the word "mandatory," as well. This word has a more forceful connotation than its synonym, "required."

When you examine sentence structure, you will find that both authors varied the lengths of sentences. The author of "Give Teens Some Work To Do!" opens with a very simple sentence to grab the attention of readers right away: "Teenagers today live in a confusing world." Later in the same paragraph, you will find the sentence, "However, as a society we should make sure that not just some, but all, teens volunteer." This sentence is not only longer than "teenagers today live in a confusing world" but far more complex grammatically. The author of the second paragraph uses the same technique, and varies sentence structure to help achieve a formal tone. This author includes additional variations in sentence structure, such as this list in the following sentence: "There are more pressures facing the modern teen than we can count: school, work, family, sports, and other extracurricular activities just to name a few."

Both authors offer logical, reasoned explanations for their points of view, and they explain their ideas carefully. Each writer uses examples and other evidence to persuade the reader. Both authors pay close attention to style and tone. This strengthens the essays and helps make them more memorable and convincing.

 PRACTICE

Review the draft of your literary analysis essay. Circle any examples in which you use the first or second person or include slang. Underline any examples

Please note that excerpts and passages in the StudySync® library and this workbook are intended as touchstones to generate interest in an author's work. The excerpts and passages do not substitute for the reading of entire texts, and StudySync® strongly recommends that students seek out and purchase the whole literary or informational work in order to experience it as the author intended. Links to online resellers are available in our digital library. In addition, complete works may be ordered through an authorized reseller by filling out and returning to StudySync® the order form enclosed in this workbook.

Reading & Writing Companion   **123**

in which you think varying the sentence structure might create a more formal style or in which you could substitute a more precise academic or domain-specific word to create a more formal tone. Provide corrections and revisions in the margins of your essay. Exchange your work with a partner and offer each other feedback.

NOTES

REVISE

CA-CCSS: CA.W.8.1a, CA.W.8.1b, CA.W.8.1c, CA.W.8.1d, CA.W.8.1e, CA.W.8.4, CA.W.8.5, CA.W.8.6, CA.W.8.9a, CA.W.8.10, CA.SL.8.1a, CA.SL.8.1c, CA.L.8.1c, CA.L.8.1d, CA.L.8.6

WRITING PROMPT

As the selections you have read in this unit show, people are shaped by their individual life experiences. People make choices, some of which are mistakes, but they often learn and grow from their experiences. Choose two selections from this unit and think about the main character or the narrator in each one. What does the main character or narrator value most, and how do the characters' experiences shape or even change their values? Write a literary analysis that shows how personal experience can change people for better or sometimes for worse.

Your literary analysis should include:

- an introduction that states a claim, or an opinion, about the theme or other aspects of one or more literary works.
- body paragraphs with relevant evidence from a literary text or texts that support the claim or opinion.
- a conclusion paragraph that follows from the body of the essay and effectively wraps up your analysis.

You have written a draft of your literary analysis and also received some feedback from your peers about how to improve it. It is time to revise your draft.

Here are some suggestions to help you revise.

- Consider the feedback you received during the peer review process.
- Examine your style throughout the essay. Be sure you have maintained a formal style. This will add credibility to your analysis and it suits your audience, which includes teachers and students.
  - › Remove any slang words or phrases.

Please note that excerpts and passages in the StudySync® library and this workbook are intended as touchstones to generate interest in an author's work. The excerpts and passages do not substitute for the reading of entire texts, and StudySync® strongly recommends that students seek out and purchase the whole literary or informational work in order to experience it as the author intended. Links to online resellers are available in our digital library. In addition, complete works may be ordered through an authorized reseller by filling out and returning to StudySync® the order form enclosed in this workbook.

Reading & Writing Companion

125

> › Locate and revise any places where you have used first or second person pronouns, such as "I," "me," "mine," "you," "your," or "yours." These pronouns are used in informal writing, giving the essay a personal and conversational style. Your literary analysis should be more formal.
> › Read through the essay once more to find and remove your personal opinions. Your essay should be clear, logical, and unbiased.

- Once you are certain the essay maintains a formal style, examine the essay's content and organization. If the answer to any of the following questions is "no," revise accordingly.

  - › Is your introduction effective, containing an interesting hook, clear thesis statement, and preview of your pain points?
  - › Does your chosen organizational structure truly suit your claim and the information you are using to support it?
  - › Consider the steps you are citing to support your claim. Does each point clearly and logically develop the claim? Does each piece of supporting information add evidence to your case?
  - › Quotations can add credibility to your case. Did you add quotations from your sources to support your claim?
  - › Examine your vocabulary choices. Are there any places where you could substitute a more precise or a more vivid word, such as an academic or domain-specific one, for a general or common one?
  - › Take a close look at the transitions you have placed between main points and paragraphs, between sentences, and between ideas. Do they clearly show the relationships you intend?
  - › Does your concluding paragraph effectively wrap up your essay by restating your thesis, summarizing your main points, and leaving readers with a lasting impression?

- Finally, read your essay with a focus on punctuation. It is very easy to change ideas or sentences while forgetting to update punctuation. Look for sentence fragments and run-ons. Pay particular attention to commas. Make sure that complex sentences are punctuated correctly.

- Check one last time for pronouns. Make sure the entire essay is in third-person to help maintain a formal style. Be sure pronouns agree with verbs in number, as well.

- Check to make sure that verb moods are consistent and make sense with the ideas you are expressing.

SKILL:
SOURCES AND
CITATIONS

⭐ DEFINE

Sources are the documents and information that authors use to research their writing. A primary source is direct evidence from a specific time and place. It includes any material that was produced by eyewitnesses to an event or who lived during an historical period. Secondary sources, in contrast, interpret and analyze primary sources. These sources are one or more steps removed from an event. Secondary sources may have pictures, quotes, or graphics from primary sources in them. Citations provide information within the text about the sources an author used to research and write a text or essay. Citations are required whenever authors quote someone else's words or refer to someone else's ideas in their writing. They let readers know who originally came up with these words and ideas. When writing a literary analysis, writers cannot simply make up information, or draw on their personal opinions or ideas. To make a convincing argument, writers must use solid research from reliable sources. If an author does not identify sources of information, the quality of the text will suffer and the writer may be accused of plagiarism.

••• IDENTIFICATION AND APPLICATION

- Sources give authors the information they need to prove their claim in an argumentative essay such as a literary analysis.

- A source should provide examples or proof that support the claim the author has made in the thesis statement.

- Sources selected by the author should be reliable primary or secondary sources. Primary sources are first-hand accounts or original materials and can include the following:

  › diaries or personal journals
  › photographs or documentary film footage
  › autobiographies
  › letters and official records

NOTES

> relics or artifacts such as pottery or clothing
> speeches

- Secondary sources interpret and analyze primary sources and can include the following:
  > online encyclopedia
  > textbooks or history books
  > magazine articles

- Authors of literary analyses should support the points they make throughout the essay by using quotations from the works they are analyzing.

- Authors should show direct quotations from a source by enclosing the exact words within quotation marks.

- A writer includes a citation to give credit to any source, whether primary or secondary, that is quoted word for word. There are several different ways to cite a source.

- One way is to put the author's last name in parenthesis at the end of the sentence in which the quote appears. This is what the writer of the Student Model essay does after every quotation. For print sources, the author's name should be followed by the page number on which the text of the quotation appears.

- Your citations can also appear as a list at the end of your essay. In the body of your essay, place a number after each reference to a primary or secondary source. At the back of your essay, list the numbers and identify the source that goes with each number.

- Citations are also necessary when a writer borrows ideas from another source, even if the writer paraphrases, or puts those ideas in his or her own words. Citations credit the source, but they also help readers discover where they can learn more.

 MODEL

The sources and citations used by the author lend credibility to a literary analysis and help prove the author's claim. Reread this section of the Student Model, "Personal Experiences: Pathways to Values," and pay particular attention to the citations used by the author.

> Both Twain and Ortiz Cofer put characters into situations that reveal their personal values. **In an excerpt from** *The Adventures of Tom Sawyer,* **readers find the main character painting a fence.** The narrator relates how unhappy Tom is with the job. **In the first paragraph of the excerpt, Tom "began to**

Copyright © BookheadEd Learning, LLC

think of the fun he had planned for this day, and his sorrows multiplied" **(Twain).** *This shows that Tom values fun more than the hard work of painting the fence.* **In Ortiz Cofer's short story, the author makes Constancia's values very clear.** *This teen-aged girl values her identity and standing in her American neighborhood far more than she values her family's Puerto Rican heritage and her grandmother's feelings.* **One illustration of this is when Constancia describes her embarrassment at being with her grandmother in public: "I try to walk far behind them in public so that no one will think we are together" (Ortiz Cofer).**

Notice how the author of the student model refers to both of the sources he used in this paragraph. He mentions Twain's book and Ortiz Cofer's short story. He includes quotations that support the points he outlines. For example, the author used the quote "began to think of the fun he had planned for this day, and his sorrows multiplied" (Twain) to show that Tom was unhappy because of his situation. He included the quote "I try to walk far behind them in public so that no one will think we are together" (Ortiz Cofer) to provide an example from "Abuela Invents the Zero" that supports the same point.

The author of the student model had to become familiar enough with the sources to find quotations that related to the claim he is making in his analysis. Quotations need to be carefully selected so that they provide examples or other support for the claim or thesis statement.

Each of these quotations includes a reference in parentheses that indicates the source author's last name after the quote. This shows that the author of the student model does not want to take credit for the ideas or the words, but rather acknowledges that they came from other sources. This is very important, because plagiarism, or copying someone else's ideas or words and claiming them as your own, is a very serious problem and can affect the essay author's credibility and even his reputation.

The next step the writer of the Student Model must take to fully give credit for his sources is to provide complete bibliographic information for *The Adventures of Tom Sawyer* and "Abuela Invents the Zero" in a Works Cited page. This Works Cited page should appear at the end of the essay and include, for each work cited in the essay, the author's name, the title of the work, the place of publication, the publisher, and the date of publication. If the work is in a collection, sometimes the name of the editor will also be included. According to Modern Language Association (MLA) style, commas are used to set off elements within each of these general groupings, but each grouping ends with a period. If a source is electronic, the last element of the citation indicates that the item is from the "Web."

Please note that excerpts and passages in the StudySync® library and this workbook are intended as touchstones to generate interest in an author's work. The excerpts and passages do not substitute for the reading of entire texts, and StudySync® strongly recommends that students seek out and purchase the whole literary or informational work in order to experience it as the author intended. Links to online resellers are available in our digital library. In addition, complete works may be ordered through an authorized reseller by filling out and returning to StudySync® the order form enclosed in this workbook.

Reading & Writing Companion   129
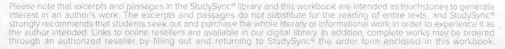

It is common practice to present the titles of full-length works such as books, plays, and movies in italics. Shorter works, such as titles of articles, chapters, speeches, short stories, poems, and songs are presented within quotation marks. If a short story is part of a collection, both the title of the short story and the title of the collection should be included in the proper format. Consider the following example:

Ortiz Cofer, Julia. "Abuela Invents the Zero." *An Island Like You: Stories of the Barrio.* Gloucester: Peter Smith Publisher, Incorporated, 1998.

You will need to search online for each text you cite in your essay and gather its complete bibliographic information. Then use this information to create a Works Cited page to accompany your essay.

 PRACTICE

Write in-text citations for quoted information in your informative essay. When you are finished, trade with a partner and offer each other feedback. How successful was the writer in citing sources for the essay? Offer each other suggestions, and remember that they are most helpful when they are constructive.

EDIT,
PROOFREAD,
AND PUBLISH

CA-CCSS: CA.W.8.1a, CA.W.8.1b, CA.W.8.1c, CA.W.8.1d, CA.W.8.1e, CA.W.8.4, CA.W.8.5, CA.W.8.6, CA.W.8.7, CA.W.8.8, CA.W.8.9a, CA.W.8.10, CA.L.8.1a, CA.L.8.1c, CA.L.8.1d, CA.L.8.2a, CA.L.8.2b, CA.L.8.6, CA.SL.8.1a, CA.SL.8.1c

WRITING PROMPT

As the selections you have read in this unit show, people are shaped by their individual life experiences. People make choices, some of which are mistakes, but they often learn and grow from their experiences. Choose two selections from this unit and think about the main character or the narrator in each one. What does the main character or narrator value most, and how do the characters' experiences shape or even change their values? Write a literary analysis that shows how personal experience can change people for better or sometimes for worse.

Your literary analysis should include:

* an introduction that states a claim, or an opinion, about the theme or other aspects of one or more literary works.
* body paragraphs with relevant evidence from a literary text or texts that support the claim or opinion.
* a conclusion paragraph that follows from the body of the essay and effectively wraps up your analysis.

The final steps to complete your literary analysis are to polish your piece by editing, proofreading, and publishing it. You should have the revised draft that you completed in a previous lesson. Think about all of the lessons in this sequence. As you reread your essay, be sure to apply what you have learned about audience and purpose, thesis statement, organization, supporting details, introductions and conclusions, transitions, style, and sources and citations. Review the suggestions that you received from the peer reviews during each step in the process and make sure you have applied them. Here are some suggestions to guide you through the process of finalizing your essay:

- Is my literary analysis essay organized effectively?

- Does my introduction grab the readers' attention in an interesting yet relevant way? Is my thesis statement part of my introduction as well as my conclusion? Does it respond to the prompt clearly and effectively and present a claim?

- Have I included strong main ideas, supporting details, and relevant evidence drawn from the texts to support my analysis and reinforce my claim?

- Have all of my sources been cited properly both within the body of my essay and in a Works Cited page at the end of my essay?

- Do I use appropriate and smooth transitions to connect ideas and details within paragraphs as well as between paragraphs?

- Have I presented my readers with a conclusion that coherently restates my thesis statement, summarizes my main ideas, and convinces readers that my argument has been fully supported?

- Have I established a formal style tone through the use of precise language and academic, domain-specific words and the elimination of slang and first or second person?

- Have I varied my sentence structure? If I read my essay out loud, does it have the right rhythm and pacing, or does it sound choppy or confusing?

- Have I incorporated all the valuable suggestions from my peers?

When you are satisfied with your work, move on to proofread it for errors. For example, check that you have used the correct punctuation for quotations and citations. Have you used ellipses to indicate where in direct quotations you have omitted material? Have you used verbals correctly? Is your use of verb moods appropriate and consistent? Are commas and dashes used appropriately? Be sure to correct any misspelled words.

Once your essay has been proofread and edited, it is time to publish your work. You can add it to your classroom's website or blog, post it on a bulletin board, or share it with family and friends. Be sure to include a list of the works you used for sources, and if you publish online, add links to those resources so that interested readers can gather more information.

Text Fulfillment Through StudySync

If you are interested in specific titles, please fill out the form below and we will check availability through our partners.

ORDER DETAILS

Date:

TITLE	AUTHOR	Paperback/ Hardcover	Specific Edition *If Applicable*	Quantity

SHIPPING INFORMATION

Contact:

Title:

School/District:

Address Line 1:

Address Line 2:

Zip or Postal Code:

Phone:

Mobile:

Email:

BILLING INFORMATION ☐ *SAME AS SHIPPING*

Contact:

Title:

School/District:

Address Line 1:

Address Line 2:

Zip or Postal Code:

Phone:

Mobile:

Email:

PAYMENT INFORMATION

☐ CREDIT CARD

Name on Card:

Card Number: Expiration Date: Security Code:

☐ PO

Purchase Order Number:

StudySync Text Fulfillment, BookheadEd Learning, LLC
610 Daniel Young Drive | Sonoma, CA 95476